DATE			
OCT 27 '76			
DEC 2 '76			
MAY 5 '77			
OCT 2 1978			
FEB 2 2 '79			
FEB 21 '84			
SEP 24 '84			

THE
FIELD
BOOK OF
MOUNTAINEERING
AND ROCK CLIMBING

THE FIELD BOOK OF MOUNTAINEERING AND ROCK CLIMBING

By Tom Lyman
with Bill Riviere

Line Drawings by Tom Lyman and Stephen Missal

Winchester Press

Library of Congress Catalog Card Number: 74-78704
ISBN: 0-87691-162-9

Published by Winchester Press
460 Park Avenue, New York 10022

PRINTED IN THE UNITED STATES OF AMERICA

Contents

THE
FIELD
BOOK OF
MOUNTAINEERING
AND ROCK CLIMBING

Atop The Eaglet at Franconia Notch, N. H., climbers are rewarded by sweeping panorama of slopes and valleys.

chapter 1
The Way to
the Mountains

Some years ago, as I walked from school in Boston, my eye was caught by a display of peculiar-looking equipment in the window of a little ski shop on Stuart Street. In one corner were a coil of rope, several pitons, a pair of climbing boots, and a carabiner. I recognized the gear for what it was, but only from pictures I'd viewed in the past. Up to that time I had never actually seen a real ice axe. A few days later I stopped by again, this time to buy a carabiner. It had been made in Austria by Stubai. Just holding it in my hand sent my mind soaring to wild and remote places. I sensed adventure in that little oval of cold steel.

*Example of unusual wildlife seen by mountaineers
in this pika in Wyoming's Grand Teton National Park.*

That summer I began hiking and climbing extensively
in Vermont and New Hampshire. I met other climbers on
the Green and White Mountain trails. I noted their equipment, talked with them about it. My first true rock climb
was on Whitehorse Ledge, a 700-foot slab of smooth granite in Conway, N.H. The ledge slopes at a fairly low angle
near the bottom, but about halfway up it becomes quite
steep where one or two tricky maneuvers are required on
very thin holds. Beyond these, the angle eases and there
follow about 200 feet of easy climbing to the gently
rounded summit. From there you can look out over the
beautiful Saco River valley and what was then the sleepy

little village of North Conway. The air was brisk, the sun bright and warm, lunch was especially tasty. Exhilaration ran through me. I was hooked on climbing.

Since that spring day, I have climbed extensively in many parts of the world, including Norway, Nepal, South America, and Alaska. Most of the world's great mountain ranges are more spectacular than New Hampshire's White Mountains but few are more beautiful. Some, like the Tetons in Wyoming, have rock formations better suited to rock climbing, plus vast splashes of colorful wild flowers. The Canadian Rockies are more remote and mysterious. The Himalayas are stupendous, with a wild beauty unequaled elsewhere. Each range has, in fact, its own special qualities, types of rock, and weather. In other words, each has a special individuality. The mountains of New England are old and rounded but they still offer challenging terrain, good rock, an abundance of trails, and there are still wild and secluded spots for those who seek them out.

Your way to the mountains begins wherever you happen to be when an interest in high, sunny, windy places first develops. While you may not want to invest the time and money necessary to acquire the experience required for climbing in the Himalayas, a knowledge of basic techniques and a moderate amount of experience will safely open up vast areas of wilderness to you, wilderness otherwise inaccessible. What's more, climbing will build up confidence in your ability to take on mentally and physically challenging situations, those in your life which might otherwise prove difficult, even overwhelming.

Few of today's activities combine the degree of physical and mental stimulation developed in climbing. Whether on a gentle slope or a steep traverse, you have direct control over your destiny. You are not an insignificant cog in a great machine, never seeing the beginning of a project, nor its end. Your ability and experience have an immediate and direct bearing on your ultimate success—or failure. You make all the decisions and take all the responsibility. You see the results of these decisions immediately. At the end of the day you may be washed out physically, but you feel a cleanliness of mind and spirit.

Climbing provides a substantial element of exploration. Even on a well-known and popular cliff, your first ascent is just that—a first ascent. It is always a thrill to stand on new ground. And it is still possible to find minor summits which are yet unclimbed, even in the United States, to say nothing of South America or Asia. Being the first to stand on a mountaintop, traverse a glacier, or cross a high pass, is no different in substance than being the first to pause at

Fig. 1. Each climber must take responsbility for safety of partners. Here, author's wife Jennifer leads party up Whitehorse Ledge at North Conway, N. H.

the North Pole or to sail around The Horn. In addition, there is much to see close at hand in the mountains. Even on routes I have hiked hundreds of times I still find fossils, rare plants, and crystals, along with other little bits of Nature strewn along the trail.

Climbing is essentially a social event, usually done in small groups. But it must not be competitive. You do not compete with the person at the other end of the rope. You work closely with him for your mutual protection and success. Contribution, not competition, is the theme. You take the ultimate responsibility for your partner's safety and welfare, and he in turn assumes that same responsibility toward you, a sort of mutual-aid pact rarely called for or possible in day-to-day life where competition in one form or another prevails. Competition between climbers can occur but usually leads to acts of bravado with climbers working beyond their ability. Grief results. The climber who introduces competition into a climb is probably in reckless pursuit of a "reputation." Climb because you enjoy it—all of it—including the rain, the cold wind, and the occasional grim bivouacs. Climbing is a team sport with little room for individual heroics.

It's important, too, never to feel that you're competing with Nature, trying foolishly to outrun a storm, for example, or shortcutting across a known treacherous slide area. Nature plays the game by her own rules and she usually wins.

A mountaineer must be prepared voluntarily to place himself under strict discipline, both mental and physical. Serious climbing requires excellent physical condition. Concentration on the task at hand is vital. You simply cannot afford to make a mistake.

Certain discomforts are to be expected, but training, physical conditioning, and, even more importantly, a sound mental discipline will see you through these discomforts with relative ease. A cold, sleepless bivouac high on a ridge may, in fact, become the memorable highlight of an entire season of climbing. Deep and long friendships have been formed or reinforced under conditions which, in other circumstances, would be considered difficult, even utterly miserable.

There are misconceptions about mountaineers and rock climbers. They are looked upon by many as daredevils who enjoy risking their necks. This is far from the case. Although climbing is occasionally dangerous, no true expert enjoys a dangerous situation. Difficult, yes, but not dangerous. A difficult route may include dangerous segments, but the two terms are not synonymous. A difficult climb can be most enjoyable, but a skilled climber avoids dangerous situations in which his control of the climb is diminished. Maneuvers that appear breathtakingly foolhardy to the uninitiated may, in fact, be routine to the expert. A difficult route requires skill, technique, and craft, and from this combination comes the enjoyment of a climb.

Misconceptions about the dangers of mountaineering usually result from accidents occurring when overeager beginners choose to skip the easy, basic-training climbs and tackle more challenging ascents before they are ready for these. Climbing above your level of ability is as dangerous as climbing on loose rock, or under an avalanche-prone slope.

During the course of several seasons, an accumulation of craft, technique, skill and mountain lore will combine to produce a competent mountaineer. Part of the joy of climbing, to me, has involved noting my own progress as I accumulated more and more skill, as I sharpened my technique and developed the mental and physical balance that made it possible for me to negotiate increasingly difficult routes.

The best conditioning for climbing, of course, is to climb. Exercise will help to tone the muscles, but if you are going to pack 50 pounds for two weeks the best conditioning is to pack 50 pounds for two weeks! No amount of running, swimming, or tennis will adequately prepare you for difficult rock climbing or for extended high-altitude ascents. Dancing and fencing are more closely related to climbing due to the requirements of good balance and the use of the feet. Gymnastics can be good, too, especially gymnastics requiring smooth execution and stressing dynamic movement. Ideally, climbing is smoothly dynamic, never static, never a series of jerks and lunges.

Another misconception is that climbers are supermen of great stamina and strength, and that climbing involves tremendous hardship. Obviously, stength is an advantage. I know several climbers who can do pull-ups with 80-pound packs on their backs. However, balance, coordination, and willpower are far more valuable assets. Mental strength and stability and the ability to relax are actually more important than brawn. Large, overdeveloped muscles can be a handicap. Using these muscles eats up large amounts of energy. And such muscles are often overworked needlessly, simply because they're there.

As climbers, women can be as skillful as men. Since they usually lack great strength in their arms and shoulders, they quickly adapt to using their legs more effectively. Frequently, too, they have a superior sense of balance and excellent stamina.

Jennifer Lyman pauses for drink and rest after strenuous climb to summit of Grand Teton in Wyoming.

Climbing demands total concentration, and this is refreshing in this day of complex thought processes involved in many sports. You direct energy and thought along one avenue and one alone—the route to the summit. Stamina, of course, is indispensable but this is often interwoven with the climber's mental outlook. A nervous person, one who can't relax, probably won't make a good climber because worrying burns up a fantastic amount of energy, resulting in physical exhaustion even during a short climb. If an emergency arises, such a climber is likely to be too tired to deal with it effectively.

During winter ascent of Middle Teton, rock outcropping protects one of author's camps from avalanches.

In short, climbing demands much but, in return, has much to offer. As a sport, it could hardly be a healthier activity. As an art, it requires the ultimate in control, finesse, and technique. And because there is always a more challenging climb waiting somewhere, you can always upgrade your skill. Also, there's little likelihood that you'll lose interest because you've "done it all."

The fusion of skill, craft, technique, and sound judgement is, in itself, a beautiful and rewarding thing, and when this is done in a setting of wind, sun, wildflowers, and ice, alone or with a few chosen companions, one of the ultimate joys of human expression is reached.

*On trail to Middle Teton, climber eats snack
to replenish energy lost through exertion and cold.*

chapter 2
Moving in
the Mountains

PACING AND THE IMPORTANCE OF RATIONING ENERGY

A climber soon learns to pace himself. This is simply the ability to get the most mileage, or altitude, from his available energy. This energy, of course, is derived from the food his body has metabolized shortly before an ascent and then during the climb. All energy supplied by a given amount of food consumed is not available immediately after digestion but rather at widely varying rates, over a period of time. How quickly depends on the food eaten and the individual's metabolism rate. If you climb at a speed that burns up energy faster than your body can produce

Hiking in Canadian Rockies, mountaineers establish relaxed, efficient pace to conserve energy.

it, or if you try to climb too long and use up your reservoir of energy, exhaustion will result.

Consider, for a moment, the relationship between mass and energy as applied to mountaineering situations. The climber and his sometimes outrageously heavy pack represent the mass which, due to inertia, will remain stationary in the valley unless acted upon by a certain force. In this case the force is applied by the legs and the energy is derived from the oxidation of candy bars, raisins, freeze-dried beef stew or other foods the climber may have eaten during the previous 24 hours or so. If the force is sustained, the mass (i.e., climber and pack) will eventually arrive at the summit. If the supply of energy fails, however, the velocity (pace) of the mass decreases to zero.

Pacing, then, is the rationing of energy being produced by the body. However, in addition to the energy required to lift yourself and your pack from the valley to the summit, several other factors will place a constant drain on your energy reserves.

For instance, energy, and a great deal of it, is required to keep your body's temperature at normal level. The colder the weather and the greater your exposure to wind and rain, the greater the drain on available energy to maintain a viable body temperature. Both the wind and rain are efficient at drawing body heat away by the processes of conduction and convection. For someone near the end of his energy reserve, this can lead to death by exposure, even at temperatures above freezing.

Tensed muscles also burn up energy. To clench your hand into a fist and then relax it requires a certain amount. Holding the fist clenched requires even more. Being forced to squint because you forgot your sunglasses requires energy, as does regaining your balance after a stumble since this activates foot, leg, and arm muscles. In such ways, a climber wastes energy unknowingly.

You can counter such waste by adopting the most relaxed muscular attitude possible, whether you're on a short day hike with a light pack, packing heavy loads over a portage, or negotiating a long, multi-pitch rock climb. Consciously relaxing all muscles except those actually needed will save substantial amounts of energy. Chances are, you'll need it later!

Another factor is the climber's mental state. Any form of mental activity consumes surprisingly large quantities of energy. Worry about a difficult route far ahead, for example, requires much more than that required for the simple evaluation of obstacles immediately ahead. Anxiety is an energy hog. Panic is even worse. It will exhaust you quickly. Obviously, then, mental relaxation conserves energy that might later be put to better use in esthetic appreciation of mountain beauty, for an extra push over the last few hundred yards to the summit, or as a reserve for an emergency.

Novice climbers sometimes forget that getting to the top is only half the project, often "blowing their energy wad" on a fast-paced ascent, only to find themselves faced with a sudden storm, increasing cold, or gathering

darkness. Then, too, there may be a long and tricky descent. Learn to pace yourself according to the requirements of the climb and your ability to handle it. You'll
then be sure of a safety-margin energy reserve.

ON WALKING

A pace is established by the speed, or rate at which you
walk or climb. As with any machine, the faster the pace,
the greater the demand on energy, with a corresponding
decrease in economy. Walking is, of course, fundamental
to climbing, and even technical rock and ice work is simply a variation on this basic series of muscular actions and
reactions. Walking efficiently conserves energy.

When walking on level ground, the foot strikes with the
heel first, then rolls forward along the sole, then pushes
off with the toe, a smooth, almost automatic process.
However, as slopes increase in steepness or where the
footing becomes uncertain, some variations of this heel-
ball-toe motion are not only possible but extremely useful.
Try to keep your feet in line, "fore and aft," avoiding a
splayed-toe duckfoot waddle or the equally unstable pi-
geon-toed stumble.

All muscles not directly engaged in walking and balance
should be completely relaxed. As slopes steepen, or for
travel on wet, slippery rocks, or possibly to guard against
stumbling in scree, additional muscles are tensed slightly
for an instant reaction should a stumble or fall occur.
("Scree" is the name given by climbers to fine gravel or
coarse dirt forming slopes or fans, below couloirs, and especially on the sides of volcanic cones.)

A fundamental variation of walking is known as the
"mountaineer's rest step." Note *step*, not stop. Place your
forward foot flat, or as flat as possible, on the slope
slightly ahead of you and swing forward and upward until
your full weight is transferred to that leg. This allows the
knee joint to lock firmly into place and momentarily
transfers your entire weight onto the bone structure of the
leg and pelvis. For a moment, the great muscles of the calf
and thigh relax completely, much as the heart muscles relax between beats. Also, because your foot is placed flat

and squarely under your center of gravity, no additional foot muscles need be tensed to maintain balance. Now, repeat with the other leg, trying to achieve a smooth, continuous action. This can be repeated almost indefinitely and when coordinated into a rhythm that includes deep and regular breathing, a good pace can be established almost automatically.

Efficiency of motion and conservation of energy are so important in climbing that anything you do to promote these will increase your chances for a safe and successful climb. Taking shorter-than-normal steps will help; so will walking around obstructions rather than stepping on or climbing over them. Plan your route with your eyes, several steps ahead, to save having to backtrack and to eliminate possible awkward and energy-consuming maneuvers. Also, a good sense of balance will minimize stumbling and the wasted exertion required for recovery.

These same principles apply when descending on rough ground, especially under a heavy pack. If the footing is in

In Norway's Jotenheimen Mountains, hikers "heel down" and take short steps as they begin descent in soft snow.

soft snow or scree, however, "heeling down" comes into play. This calls for kicking the heels vigorously into the yielding surface, creating a small step which supports the foot. This method, also known as the "plunge step," frequently provides the quickest and most efficient descent. Be sure to keep your knees slightly flexed, in case you encounter a rock or other firm surface immediately below the scree. Coming down hard, under the added momentum of descent with a heavy pack, could be dangerous to the knees if they are locked rigidly straight. Heeling down can be fun but don't yield to the temptation to run. Scree and snow slopes can be steep enough to provide a bad tumble if you trip.

CARE OF THE FEET

"My feet are killing me!" How many times have I heard this lament, usually a couple of miles out on a 10-mile trek. The feet are the least appreciated and most abused parts of the body, yet for a climber they are the most vital element affecting mobility and enjoyment.

Feet should be kept scrupulously clean. Proper hygiene calls for frequent washing with soap, close trimming of the toenails, and immediate attention to any blisters or chafing. During long climbs or on expeditions where boots and the same socks may be worn for several days, a medicated powder such as Dr. Scholl's should be applied liberally and regularly. Frequent changes to clean socks will add comfort and hygiene to the enjoyment of a climb, and may even add substantially to the distance covered during a given day.

Take advantage of rest stops where you can remove your boots and socks to air your feet. If possible, wash them in a brook or pond but don't soak them at length. Even cold water tends to soften the skin, subsequently leading to blisters. Dip the feet quickly in and out of the water to stimulate circulation. Whether you may choose to take a full-body dip depends, of course, on the relative air and water temperatures.

Air-dry your feet in sunlight, if possible. At higher altitudes, even a few minutes' exposure will allow the sun's ultraviolet rays to kill bacteria common to sweaty climbing boots and on feet. Turn your socks inside out, spreading them in the sun to dry. Open your boots, too, and place them so that sunlight and fresh air will penetrate their interior as much as possible. Ten minutes of this therapy will go a long way toward keeping feet healthy and comfortable.

The need for keeping toenails closely trimmed is not vital during an ascent. But during your descent, excessively long nails may cause severe pain as they are rammed into the toe of the boot with each step. Even the best-fitting boot allows the foot to slide forward slightly, and if the boot is too short or the toenails are too long, misery results. I've met climbers walking backward down a trail, seeking to relieve the anguish that accompanied each step. The loss of toenails from this cause is not only extremely painful but may make further walking impossible.

On rough ground, as in Jotenheimen Mountains, blisters and fatigue can be avoided by proper foot care.

Blisters are a common problem; even the most experienced climbers are plagued by them (occasionally). They can usually be avoided, however, even when breaking in a new pair of stiff boots. Immediately attend to any chafing or "hot spots." If a blister does form, avoid breaking it unless it puffs up so badly that it obviously should be drained. Any opening in the skin, especially on the foot, is highly vulnerable to infection. Miles from civilization, however, you may be forced to aggravate a blister by walking out. This, needless to say, is at the risk of serious infection which may later require massive doses of antibiotics, to say nothing of being laid up, possibly for several weeks. In British Columbia I once came across a climber literally crawling down a remote trail on his hands and knees. His partner carried two packs. Attached to one of them was a pair of nearly new, heavy climbing boots. After applying an antibiotic cream and a topical ointment to ease the pain, we carried the victim to the highway, then drove him to a doctor in Banff. The details of his problem were obvious. He had purchased the boots through the mail only a few days before undertaking the trip. He had failed to toughen his feet with a few preliminary jaunts and he overlooked properly breaking in the new boots. The only practical cure for blisters is prevention!

Pressure on a hot spot or blister can sometimes be relieved by fashioning a doughnut-shaped piece of moleskin, placing the hole over the blister, then covering the entire area with a larger piece of moleskin. In an emergency, adhesive tape or an adhesive bandage will do. Better yet, never go into the mountains without a supply of moleskin.

Despite ounces (and pounds) of prevention, however, blisters will balloon—puff up to the extent that they must be broken and drained. Otherwise they'll break on their own, inviting infection. Wash the area thoroughly, then daub it with antiseptic. With a match flame sterilize the point of any sharp-pointed instrument—a needle is best, the point of a knife second choice. Puncture the blister at the side, not on top, and carefully squeeze the liquid out. Re-apply antiseptic and cover with a sterile bandage. For added protection and comfort, overlay the bandage generously with moleskin. Oxygen is important to the elimination of infectious organisms, so expose the blister to fresh air during rest stops.

Keep your feet as dry as possible, especially in temperatures ranging from just above to just below freezing. Prolonged wet feet can result in numbness which makes walking difficult and climbing dangerous. Wash your socks daily in mild weather, drying one pair on your pack as you travel. When drying boots, don't prop them close to a roaring fire. Quick, excessive heat will shrink the leather, turn it hard and brittle, and make the boots almost impossible to put on and wear. Dry them as well as possible with a gentle heat, some distance from the fire. Even if they don't dry thoroughly, wool socks will cushion your feet from remaining dampness.

Treat your feet right. They're your only means of travel in the mountains.

New Hampshire Andean Expedition experienced this view of Nevado Ranrapalca, Cordillera Blanca, in Peru.

chapter 3
Some Thoughts from the Mountains

Suitable equipment will allow a mountaineer to climb efficiently in safety and camp in reasonable comfort with a minimal threat to the environment. It must be realistically lightweight, effective, and durable, absolutely of the highest quality to withstand the severest climatic and climbing situations. Anything short of these standards is out of the question. If it is esthetically attractive, so much the better; there is no need to accept visually offensive gear, and the good stuff is generally pleasing to the eye.

The old-time woodsman is still admired for his ability to get around in the outdoors by making do with natural materials at hand. However, in the high country above timberline, his skills would be of little practical value, although he'd be a useful member of the party approaching a mountain through wooded country—and as a resourceful back-up man in an emergency. Most well-known, and heavily traveled mountain areas today could not withstand the old-time techniques. High-elevation plant and animal communities, already handicapped by poor soils, short growing seasons, thin growth and population, simply cannot tolerate great numbers of people using an axe to erect lean-tos, build bough beds, or even make campfires! This is true both of higher altitudes and high latitudes. Mountaineers in subpolar regions must sometimes cross miles of fragile tundra and they are expected to use extreme care not to inflict permanent damage or scars upon the landscape, or to interfere with wildlife, or to hinder struggling communities of rare plants.

This does not mean that you can never enjoy a campfire or supplement your diet with a few trout. In truly remote areas where wood is plentiful, a campfire is appropriate, and it's one of life's few remaining simple pleasures. Modern society likes rules of thumb, thus minimizing the need for individual judgement. A good rule of thumb regarding campfires is to build one only on mineral soil—sand or gravel—or on solid rock, and only if there is ample water at hand to extinguish it or wet sand or gravel to bury it. Fire built on humus or sphagnum-moss soils can smolder for days without telltale smoke, later breaking out to run wild. Dead wood means a cleaner flame, less smoke and soot, than green growth. Driftwood on the shores of lakes and rivers is usually excellent fuel and, of course, the water's edge is generally safe for a campfire. And remember the old adage: "Indian gets warm with small fire; white man gets warm chopping wood."

Be sure it is dead out before leaving it. Pour water on it until the ashes float; turn over and wet down individual sticks that may still be smoldering. If you're unable to find an absolutely safe spot for a campfire, forego it. Picturesque deadwood found near mountain tarns should not be disturbed, certainly not burned as firewood. This is part of the natural scene and will eventually help replenish nutrients in the soil.

Fish are a renewable resource and can improve the unexciting diet common to climbing trips in remote areas. There are several pack-type fly and spinning rods that break down into short sections, as little as 18 to 20 inches long. Reels are light and compact, lures almost weightless. Take only the fish you need, preferably from larger lakes and streams, leaving the tiny mountain tarns or rivulets undisturbed. Small ponds and streams cannot stand

On Yellowstone River, Tom Lyman uses pack-type fly rod to add sport and vary his menu on long climbing trip.

heavy fishing pressure, soon becoming fished out. Large groups should forego fishing and certainly they shouldn't try to feed themselves, even partially, by scavenging from meadows and ponds. Practicing so-called "survival" techniques is utterly ludicrous and wasteful.

Suitable equipment and supplies will allow you to operate independently of the environment. Carrying your own shelter, food, stove and fuel, in addition to climbing gear, should not burden you unduly, although during extensive expeditions heavy packs and numerous relays are usually necessary. As for your own outfit, once you have packed the essentials, additional and burdensome weight results from adding "comfort" items, extra food, or other nonessentials. Safety dictates a repair kit and selected items

American Dhaulagiri Expedition of 1973 saw memorable sunset bathe majestic crags of Annapurna I.

of extra food and clothing for emergencies, but don't overdo it. An expert's pack rigged for a two-week trip often weighs less than that of a beginner on a weekend jaunt.

Consider, too, the growing problem of trash piles. Avoid as much as possible carrying anything that will end up as rubbish. Food wrappings and containers serve no other function; some are necessary but many can be eliminated by careful and ingenious repacking before leaving home. Plastic bags are ideal for such repacking, especially for bulk foods like flour, sugar, macaroni, freeze-dried vegetables whose cardboard and paper containers can be eliminated in favor of more convenient package sizes. Metal cans are virtually indestructible and must be packed out. Glass bottles are absurd. Nothing a backpacker needs requires a glass container—not even catsup, which is now available in tiny packets.

If you choose a butane or propane stove, remember that the empty cartridges must be toted out. They are bulky, and in the case of propane they weigh almost as much empty as full. Consider gasoline for stove fuel. It is less expensive, more efficient, and obtainable almost anywhere in the world. Lightweight aluminum canteens are suitable as containers. *Carry out everything you've carried in.*

With regard to equipment, too much emphasis has been directed to the "newest," the "lightest," *ad nauseam.* The result is a loss of perspective as to what climbing is all about. This Madison Avenue type of huckstering has resulted in the "equipment freak" who owns seven different packs of nearly similar design, four virtually alike sleeping bags, and at least three ice axes, pristine and shiny. He's been too busy collecting gear to use it! There's nothing wrong with accumulating equipment, but accumulating is not climbing! The true expert owns what he needs, and he uses it. Skill comes from doing, not from poring through catalogs and memorizing specifications.

On New Hampshire's Cannon Mountain, author's wife proves that backpack doesn't impede experienced climber.

chapter 4
It's All
on Your Back

Packs and rucksacks, sometimes called knapsacks, are probably available in a wider variety of designs, materials, and sizes than any other item of gear used by mountaineers. What's more, even experienced climbers often choose a pack on the basis of color, brand name, or the maker's reputation, rather than design and structural refinements.

For one-day hikes and technical climbing, a small, frameless rucksack which hangs directly from the shoulders is usually adequate. It's capacity is limited, however, even if the pouch is fairly large. I prefer a pack that is a little longer and narrower so that no part of it extends to

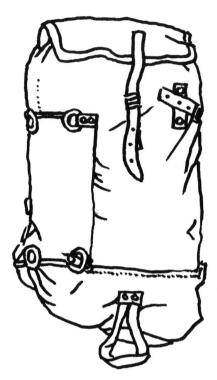

Fig. 2. This is "guide's pack," or technical rock climbing pack; note narrow shape and absence of exterior pockets that might get snagged.

the sides to catch on brush or to hang me up in a tight chimney. For rock climbing, the pack should have no outside pockets. Unfortunately, even the best packs often are rigged with exterior loops for an ice axe, and with straps to hold crampons, ropes and other paraphernalia. Designers seem bent upon having a climber display his equipment rather than carry it securely. These exterior loops and straps increase the chance of losing gear, and they can snag on ledges and rock projections. If you need greater capacity, don't attach your equipment to the outside of your pack. Instead, buy a larger one.

For rock climbing a waist strap is indispensable. This keeps the pack close to the body and prevents the load from shifting to either side. In the event of a fall, it may also prevent loss of the pack.

As for the fabric that goes into a pack, canvas is preferable to nylon for rock climbing because it better resists wear and abrasion on rough rock surfaces. It is heavier than nylon but not significantly so. The pack should be as light as possible without sacrificing durability and strength. It makes little sense to carry six pounds of gear in a seven-pound pack! A double layer of fabric should reinforce the bottom, and this, along with the top flap, should be waterproof.

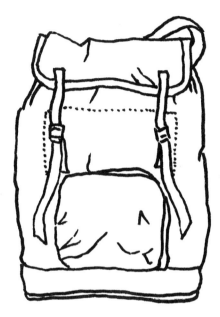

Fig., 3. This is light knapsack of type usually designated "day pack." Frameless nylon or canvas pouch is compact and has reinforcement of leather at bottom.

Check the pack's hardware and fittings. They should be durable, preferably nickel-plated. Shoulder straps may or may not be padded, although for heavier loads thinly padded straps offer some comfort. The upper end of the shoulder straps must be attached to the center of the pack, directly behind the neck. This helps center the pack on the body, minimizing side-shift.

A metal hauling ring or a stout nylon loop is useful, too, attached so that you can clip the pack to a piton or other anchor in an upright position on a steep wall, or for hauling it up over a difficult pitch.

For longer, alpine-type climbs or extended hikes, large frameless packs are often used. But a better choice is one incorporating a light, somewhat flexible frame of aluminum rod, fiberglass, or thin stainless steel. Such a pack better distributes weight and makes heavier loads more comfortable. If the pouch can be easily removed from the frame, so much the better. It can then be stored or carried separately if necessary. On expedition-type climbs where

*Author, wearing full climbing pack, works his way
along Slabs of Lethe Route on Cannon Mountain.*

heavily laden rigid-frame packs are used to carry supplies
to a given point, the smaller, flexible-framed rucksacks
are often used for relaying gear to a higher camp or over
difficult terrain. Unless it is overloaded, a rucksack is the
type most easily kept in balance on steep rock or ice.

Some more elaborate flexible-frame packs have several
interior and exterior pockets, and often include reinforced

Fig. 4. This is large-size rucksack for ski-mountaineering. Behind side pockets it has reinforced channels to carry skis.

channels for carrying skis. There may even be a sleeve of waterproof material that can be unfurled so that, in biv-ouac, a climber can pull this sleeve up over his legs while his feet are inserted into the pack for extra warmth! Sleeve or no sleeve, the cover flap should be cut gener-ously enough so that it fully protects the bag's contents, even when the pack is overflowing. Generally speaking, the longer and narrower this type of bag is, the better adapted it is to climbing since it does not impede the use of a climber's arms. Incidentally, when carrying crampons inside a pack, the sharp points can be disarmed by im-bedding them in "spider" protectors.

The rigid, tubular aluminum packframe, contoured to fit a person's back, and equipped with a commodious, usually well-designed and brilliantly colored nylon bag, has virtually replaced all other types of packs for carrying heavy loads. This pack is designed so that the bulk of the weight is placed high and close to the body, and so that the weight is carried not by the shoulders but the hips, pelvic structure, and the legs. Such a pack is far less tiring than one which pulls at the shoulders and tends to throw a packer off balance to the rear. With this updated design you can walk erect, and breathing is nearer normal.

What's more, you can enjoy the scenery, rather than being forced to lean forward with only the trail immediately ahead in view.

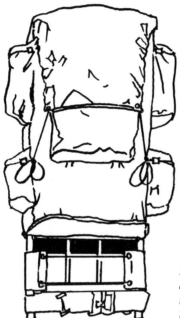

Fig. 5. This is tubular aluminum packframe holding typical expedition-style bag of tough but light nylon.

When shopping for a packframe of this type, ask the salesperson if you can place it on the floor and put your full weight on it. If the clerk is reluctant, buy your pack elsewhere. Under this test, a good frame will flex slightly but it won't break. Aluminum packframes should be welded by the heli-arc method which produces the strongest possible weld. This is a high-frequency welding method, accomplished in an atmosphere of inert gas which prevents surface blemishes and brittleness. Check to see that all holes and fittings are neatly drilled and properly aligned. Be sure, too, that the frame is not warped. If end plugs are missing, insist that they be replaced. They can be secured permanently with epoxy. And, of course, don't make any modifications in the frame if there is a chance that you may want to exchange it for a larger size or different model.

Good pouch construction is important, too. See that it fits the frame closely and is attached by clevis pins and key wires, rather than with a series of fingernail-breaking split rings. This makes it easier to remove the pouch for toting unusually heavy or bulky loads. Examine all fabric seams closely for sloppy sewing.

Some bags used on this type of frame are truly immense—up to 4,000 cubic inches or more, as compared to 1,000 to 2,000 cubic inches typical of day packs. The larger bags are generally for expeditionary use. They are of little advantage for average treks. In fact, buying too large a pouch encourages careless packing and loads too heavy for short trips. If additional capacity becomes necessary, an extension unit is available to raise the height of the frame. This makes most frames adaptable to a variety of uses.

Belt pouches and waist packs are at their best with small loads, up to five or six pounds, and are handy for such items as a first-aid kit, camera and film, maps, lunch, and sunglasses. Carrying oft-needed personal items such as lip and sunburn creams in such a pack eliminates rummaging around in a larger pack. A belt-pouch zipper should be installed at the top, not along the side, so that contents don't spill when the bag is opened. Be sure the zipper works smoothly. Tug on the belt loops to make sure they are firmly attached.

If weight is properly distributed over shoulders and back, large loads can be carried to base camps with relative ease. Climber is toting load through ice-fall on American Dhaulagiri Expedition.

*Climbers prepare to unload gear for night's stay
on West Buttress of Mount Logan in Yukon Territory.*

chapter 5
Enjoying
the Nights, Too

SLEEPING BAGS

There is little about a sleeping bag that is mysterious. Its
prime function is to retain natural body warmth. It does
not *make* you warm but, rather, prevents the heat of your
body from escaping.

It achieves this by means of dead-air space trapped in
the filler which, in itself, is also a poor conductor of heat.
The colder the ambient temperature, the greater the exposure to wind, the more marked the radiation of the earth's
warmth (as on a cool, clear night as opposed to a warm,
cloudy atmosphere), the more dead-air space is required

to keep you comfortable. The degree of warmth, then, is governed by the fluffed-up thickness of the filler, known as "loft." Bags used in cold weather are capable of three, four, five, even 10 inches of loft. Yet, when such bags are stuffed for packing, they must be reasonably compact bundles. And, of course, they must be lightweight.

Eiderdown is lightest but not as durable as goose down which, because of its compressibility, lofting qualities, and light weight, is commonly used in virtually all sleeping bags carried by mountaineers. There is no noticeable difference between gray and white goose down. White is more expensive simply because it is rarer, not warmer. Duck down, used in less expensive bags, does not loft as well because it is heavier and its filaments shorter. Also, feathers are frequently included in so-called "duck-down" sleeping bags. Some excellent bags feature a combination of duck and goose down, considered an advantage by some climbers who believe that the more resilient and stouter duck-down fibers increase durability. It's a moot point.

If you plan to take up serious climbing and mountaineering with the possibility of extensive treks, buy the very best goose-down sleeping bag you can afford. Don't appraise the various bags according to the number of pounds of down inserted into the bag. What counts is the loft, or thickness of insulation that surrounds you when the bag is unfurled.

Until recently, no man-made fillers even approximated the efficiency of natural down. True, they insulated as well (three inches of fiberglass or steel wool has about the same insulation values as down) but only down combined the necessary compressibility, loft, and lightness. Synthetic fillers could not be compressed for packing, they were heavy, and their lofting qualities left much to be desired. Such synthetics did become popular, but only among car campers to whom weight and bulk are not handicaps.

However, a more recent development, Dacron Fiberfill II, is fast closing the gap between natural down and synthetics. Fiberfill II will compress about 90 percent as much as down. And to equal the loft provided by one pound of down, it takes only 1.4 pounds of Fiberfill II. Also, the latter maintains its uniformity when wet, whereas down lumps, loses insulation value, is slow to dry. Finally, Fiberfill II is considerably less expensive than down.

I am by no means claiming that even the best synthetics can match the efficiency of down. For mountaineering, nothing can equal high-grade goose down as a sleeping-bag filler. However, it is obvious that technology may, one of these days, crowd down out of the picture. Each new synthetic product comes closer to that goal.

In the meantime, certain techniques further increase the efficiency of a down sleeping bag. For instance, it should not be rolled or folded for packing. This is time-consuming. Worse yet, repeated folding or rolling along the same lines tends to damage the down. Instead, the bag should be stuffed into a nylon sack, one usually provided

Fig. 6. These down sleeping bags—Eddie Bauer brand (top) and Comfy brand Mt. Whitney Model—both feature drawstring hood and full-length side zipper.

with a sleeping bag. Once in camp, the bag should be "un-stuffed" and laid out to fluff out to full loft. This can be speeded up by shaking the bag and fluffing it with the hands. Down filaments are resilient and, unless wet, will spring back into shape to p᠆ ɔduce full loft, even after re-peated compressions. Small amounts of static electricity help this lofting process by building up charges on each filament, repelling those around it.

Sleeping-bag construction is also intended to aid this lofting process. For instance, the outer shell should be

Fig. 7. Diagrams show details of sleeping-bag construction discussed in text: (1) quilted type—sewn through—may allow cold spots between down-filled compartments; (2) double quilt is an improvement; (3 and 4) box and slant box are also warmer than single quilted type; (5) overlapping tubes, favored by author, provide very efficient insulation; (6) cross-section of bag shows down-filled baffle (A) over zipper, plus differential cut of liner (B) and larger shell (C), while second cross-section (7) shows use of foam pad to compensate when bag is compressed by sleeper's weight.

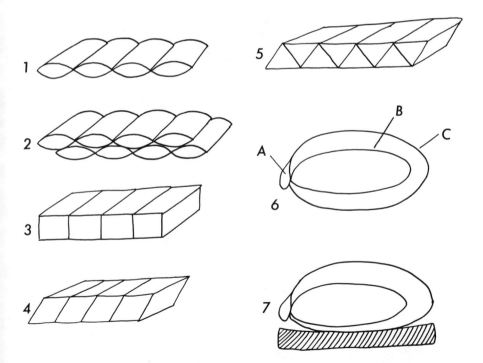

larger than the inner lining; this is known as a "differential cut." In between these inner and outer surfaces are boxes or tubes into which the down is blown, and which serve to keep it from shifting and causing cold spots. Baffles, separating the boxes or tubes, are usually of a mesh-like fabric. The better sleeping bags have these baffles sewed in so that the tubes overlap. The size of these limits the amount of loft achieved by the down so that too much down will only make the bag heavier, not necessarily warmer.

Nylon has replaced all other fabrics that go into the making of the envelope, or shell. Being light, strong, and so tightly woven that down cannot escape through the weave, nylon is ideal. Also, because it is slippery, it eases the chore of stuffing the bag into a small stuff-sack. For this reason, too, you can twist and turn in the bag without getting tangled in the lining.

A hood with a drawstring to enclose the shoulders and head in cold weather is standard on the better bags. A small cord clamp will keep the drawstring securely closed. A small piece of Velcro tape attached to the upper end of the zipper helps maintain a tight closure.

Look for at least a No. 10, toothed, nylon zipper. Coil zippers have not proven as trouble-free as the toothed type. The zipper should be full-length, and it should run along one side of the bag so that it can be partially opened without fully exposing the sleeper. Most bags are available with either a right- or left-side slide fastener, allowing two bags to be zipped together. A second slider, at the foot of the bag, will allow for cooling the feet without having to open the bag fully. A down-filled tube, acting as an air baffle behind the zipper, will prevent the escape of warmth through this.

For use in extreme cold where a sufficient thickness of down must be maintained about the feet, some sleeping bags incorporate fabric stiffeners; others have a built-in bulge, a sort of foot compartment. The mummy-shaped bag is standard for mountaineering because its body contour reduces open air space inside. Also, the mummy shape is lighter than either the rectangular or the barrel-shaped bag of comparable loft.

Try to keep the bag clean. In time, it will get soiled, but a down bag can be washed by hand or in a machine with a delicate-fabric setting. Use only mild soap in lukewarm water, never a detergent. The bag must be rinsed thoroughly to remove all traces of soap film which might otherwise act as a wetting agent, causing the fabric to wet more readily when exposed to rain or snow. Draw water from the sleeping bag as well as possible by wrapping it in dry turkish towels, then place it in a tumble-dry machine. Do this carefully. Rough handling may tear the interior baffles. Dry with moderate heat. This will require many cycles. Never use higher heat settings to speed the process. A pair of rubber tennis shoes, tumbled with the bag during the latter stages of drying, will help break up the clots of down which tend to stick together. This also generates static electricity, causing the down to fluff more readily.

Oil and grease stains are best removed by dry cleaning but this should be done only by a cleaning firm familiar with down sleeping bags or down-filled garments. Stoddard solvent is used by most such dry cleaners. Other types of cleaning fluids will remove the natural oil from the down filaments, causing them to become brittle and shortening their useful life considerably.

If only a few spots are to be removed, have the bag spot-cleaned, then wash to remove the residue of dirt and cleaning fluids. However, if the bag is completely dry-cleaned, it must be aired thoroughly, preferably by hanging it loosely in the sun and wind for at least a half-day to remove all traces of fluid. Vapors from this have proven fatal in several instances, when campers have slept in bags recently dry-cleaned but not properly aired. The fluid is also highly flammable and a spark may cause the bag to explode if vapor traces remain. Never use coin-operated dry-cleaning machines. A good down sleeping bag deserves professional treatment.

As for sleeping bags insulated with Dacron Fiberfill II, these can be washed easily in the conventional manner in any washing machine and dried in a tumble drier with equal ease.

Any sleeping bag, but especially a down-filled one, should be stored loosely, preferably unrolled, in a warm, dry place.

FOAM PADS

Often overlooked by beginners is the fact that body weight will compress the down. Loft disappears, eliminating dead-air space. You may be in for a cold night's sleep, even with the thickest down bag, unless supplementary insulation is used underneath. This also provides cushioning against the hard ground.

Air mattresses and foam pads accomplish this. Foam has several advantages over air. It needs no inflating at night, nor deflating in the morning. Neither will it leak. (It's surprising how little abrasion it takes to puncture some air mattresses!) What's more, an air mattress provides a colder bed since air in the tubes can circulate freely, drawing heat from the body by convection.

A closed-cell foam pad resists soaking up ground moisture and restricts heat loss by convection since the cells do not interconnect. The pad should be covered with a waterproof fabric shell; coated nylon is often used for this. A full-length pad, 1¼ inches thick, is only slightly heavier and bulkier than the so-called shorty or "hiker's model," usually only 48 inches long. A full pad provides warmth and comfort for the entire body, including the feet. A good night's sleep is important when serious climbing awaits you in the morning.

*Author used this roomy double A-frame tent while
camping on Klutland Glacier in Alaska.*

chapter 6
Tenting Tonight

TENTS

In most parts of the world a tent is a virtual necessity when climbing at moderate to high altitudes. It serves as protection against wind, rain, snow; helps contain body and artificial heat and, on extended climbs, provides a place to eat and to socialize. It keeps small vermin, mosquitoes, black flies, and other insects at bay. Each of these functions affects the design of a mountain tent.

Only three basic types, however, are truly useful to mountaineers. These are the A-frame tent, the Logan, and the exterior-frame type, with some variations in each category.

Climbers are shown setting up light backpacking tent and opening down-insulated arctic-type sleeping bags.

The A-Frame Tent: This is the simplest design, not un-like a pup tent in general appearance, but much more so-phisticated. Usually available as a two-man shelter, it is easily erected by assembling poles at each end and it may be guyed to stakes, rocks, or even an ice axe imbedded in the snow. In confined situations—on narrow ledges, be-neath overhanging rocks, or where a tent platform must be dug in the snow, the A-frame, two-man model is gener-ally preferable. Its steeply sloping sides shed snow better than most other tents, and its low profile presents minimal resistance to high winds. These advantages are slightly offset by a lack of interior space, notably headroom.

*Fig. 8. Typical two-man mountain tent has A-frame
design and features snow flaps and shock cords.*

Overall quality is important in all tents but there are
specific features you should seek in an A-frame for mountain use. It should have at least one "tunnel entrance," for
instance: a fabric sleeve, two to four feet long, large
enough for a man to crawl through from the outside into
the tent. This sort of entryway acts as a baffle which keeps
wind and snow out as climbers enter or exit.

The tent's ridge line should be a catenary cut, the drape
or curve that occurs when any wire, rope, or fabric is suspended between two points. It is impossible to eliminate
this sag entirely, and if the tent fabric is cut to accommodate it, few if any wrinkles will develop as the walls are
pulled taut. This, then, distributes strain evenly—no one
point bears the brunt—and reduces the tent's tendency to
flap in the wind. Incidentally, continued flapping can become most annoying, can even make sound sleep difficult. Also, loose fabric contributes to heat loss by convection as air currents are moved about inside the shelter.
Ideally, the air inside a tent should be calm, even with a
gale blowing outside. The catenary cut contributes to this
interior calmness.

The floor should be one thickness of tough, waterproof
fabric extending at least 14 inches up the walls; 18 inches
is better. This is known as a "tub bottom." The tent should
provide at least 7½ square feet per person unless designed

with a vestibule where equipment can be stored. A zippered "cook hole" in the floor makes it possible to set the stove on an exterior surface, preventing damage to the fabric by the stove's heat as well as eliminating spills inside the tent.

If the poles are connected by elastic shock cord, they are less likely to get lost and will be held together more securely as the frame and tent flex in the wind. Zippers should be of nylon, of the toothed type, and easily replaceable. A ventilator at each end, one that can be closed with a drawstring, will assure fresh air, yet can be closed against a slashing storm. And, naturally, all openings should be protected with insect netting.

The Logan Tent: The Logan tent is usually a large shelter with an interior center pole, patterned after a design proven in the Arctic and on climbing expeditions all over the world. Originally of heavy canvas, it served especially well as a cooking, storage, and communal shelter at base camps. Some military mountain tents in use today are of this design. Modern Logan-type tents normally sleep four

Fig. 9. Logan design has center pole, with guy lines running from peak to stabilize tent in high winds.

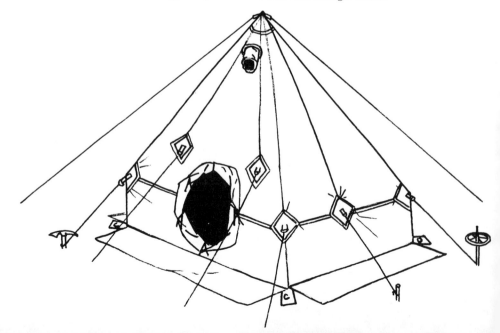

persons—more in a pinch. They are made of nylon, and suspended on a sectionalized or telescoping aluminum center pole.

Some problems accompany the roominess of the Logan. Its large fabric surfaces are highly vulnerable to winds, resulting in great stress against the fabric at the peak and at other suspension points. Because of this, all corners, pull-out tabs, and seams should be well stitched and heavily reinforced. The pole must go together easily and should be equipped with a wide base plate to prevent damage to the floor fabric. Low vertical walls are typical of the Logan but these should be at least 18 inches high and waterproof. Ordinarily the tent is equipped with a tunnel entrance but some of these are ridiculously small and difficult to negotiate, especially when you're wearing a heavy parka.

Exterior-Frame Tent: There are several variations of this design, most of them available in two-, four-, six-, and eight-man styles. The Blanchard design is a rectangular shelter with poles and metal parts of aluminum. The best example of this model is the Bishop's Ultimate tent made

Fig. 10. Author considers this Bishop's Ultimate
model best example of exterior-frame Blanchard design.

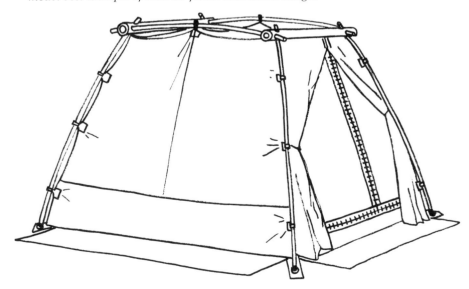

for two or four persons. The suspension system is rugged, interior space is ample, and the tent is relatively easy to erect, even when anchor points for guying are inadequate or lacking.

Another exterior-frame tent which has proven its worth on several major expeditions, including the American Dhaulagiri Expedition in 1973, is the Kelwood tent of the hoop or barrel design. It looks not unlike a covered-wagon top or a Quonset hut, the frame usually of fiberglass, inserted into exterior sleeves. It is quite roomy, and although it presents a sizeable profile to the wind, the resiliency of the fiberglass poles reduces flapping and strain on the fabric.

Here again, of course, quality of materials and workmanship is critical. Be sure, too, that the poles and various sections of hardware comprising the frame are not so

This double A-frame has been pitched in soft snow, with snowshoes and ice axes serving as anchors.

complex that setting up the tent under difficult or stormy conditions will be next to impossible. Such frames often include 12 or more sections and, if one is missing, the frame cannot be erected. Better that the pole sections be interchangeable. You can then carry one or two spares, since it is very difficult to set up such a tent by improvising a jerry rig. It can be done but is rarely satisfactory. An A-frame tent can be set up by substituting a ski pole, ice axe, or willow wands for a broken or missing pole section but this is not possible with the more complex exterior frame.

Unfortunately, most exterior-frame tents are usually equipped with inadequate zippers. If you like the tent but not the zippers, have them replaced. Their failure in the field can be annoying—and dangerous.

All suitable mountain tents are designed to give somewhat in the wind, with their frames made flexible to minimize strain on fabric from wind, or the weight of snow. An exception is the Whillan's Box, really a portable hut with heavy, rigid frame and a flat roof. It has limited value for weekend climbers but on long expeditions, where weight is not critical, the "box" provides effective shelter.

Almost all mountain tents on the market are copies or modifications of those I've described. However, not all are useful in every situation. When buying a tent, consider the type of climbing you'll be doing, and the weather conditions you're likely to encounter. Severe conditions of weather or terrain require special tents which may not be practical for average weekend use, or may be too expensive. When dependency on your tent is important, avoid experimental or revolutionary designs. These must be tested thoroughly before they are committed to a difficult climb. Severe damage or loss of a tent can be disastrous.

TENT FLIES

If vapor given off by breathing and cooking cannot pass effectively into the outdoors through the fabric of your tent, interior condensation results. In warm weather, water will gather in puddles. In winter climates, ice will form inside.

A tent fabric cannot be both "breathable" (i.e. allow the outward passage of interior moisture), and waterproof to protect you and your gear against slashing rain or melting snow. The only effective solution so far developed is to use a separate, waterproof fly. Thus, inside moisture can escape through the tent fabric into the air between the tent and fly, but rain cannot penetrate the latter. The fly should be suspended a few inches above the tent but at no point touching it. The fly for a center-pole or exterior-frame tent should be shaped to conform to the contours of the tent, with adequate tabs for hold-down cords, to prevent its being blown away.

SPECIAL EQUIPMENT FOR TENTS

Have *snow flaps* installed on your tent if it is not so equipped. These are fabric strips, preferably waterproof, 12 to 16 inches wide, sewed along the bottom of the tent walls.

Fig. 11. Detail drawing shows how to install elastic shock cord in tent's guy line.

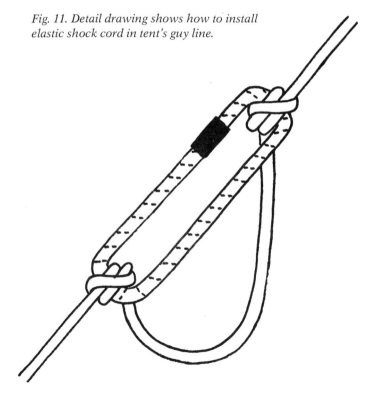

They are the counterparts of the "sod cloth" used on old-time floorless wall tents. Laid flat on the ground, outside the tent of course, snow is then piled on them to help secure the tent against wind and to make the shelter generally more stable. They also help to keep the floor squared if stakes fail to hold in the snow. Rocks or sod can be used on the snow flaps when the tent is pitched on bare ground.

Every mountain tent should have *shock cords,* small loops of elastic line attached to guy lines to absorb the shock of buffeting by strong winds. Each guy line or pull-out tab line should be equipped with one of these. As an added bonus, they reduce flapping, and they take up the shock should someone trip over a guy line.

Well-equipped climber pauses on Mount Logan, at 17,000 feet, to view Mount Augusta in Yukon Territory.

chapter 7
Vital Odds and Ends

STOVES AND FUELS

A mountaineer in the field spends most of his time above timberline, and his camps are likely to be where there is no natural fuel. Hence the wide variety of small, portable stoves which burn liquid fuels, most of which are designed for backpacking and mountain travel.

Choice is generally based on the fuel rather than on the stove. Fuels include propane, butane, alcohol, gasoline, and kerosene (known as "paraffin" in Europe). Alcohol is generally unsuited since it fails to produce adequate heat for cold-weather or high-altitude cooking. Propane and butane are perhaps the most convenient and the cleanest, since these come packaged in disposable cans or cylinders which are screwed directly into appropriate stoves. The two are considered the safest to handle, yet they can be dangerous.

On the American Dhaulagiri Expedition in 1973, I destroyed an eight-man base-camp tent by attempting to change a butane cartridge in the shelter while a second stove burned. In the thin air of 19,000 feet, I probably wasn't thinking clearly and I failed to insert the new cartridge properly. It leaked. There was an explosion. The several men in the tent with me scrambled for the exits. No one was hurt, but the tent was a total loss. Neither the fuel nor the packaging was to blame. This was a case of carelessness. Butane and propane have a good safety record. However, they do have a serious drawback: The empty cans and cylinders must be carried out for disposal. Having carried them in full, many climbers are loath to tote them out empty. Litter results. For this reason alone, I have stopped using these gases on climbing trips.

Kerosene provides greater BTU[1] potential, is less volatile than butane or propane, and there are a few excel-

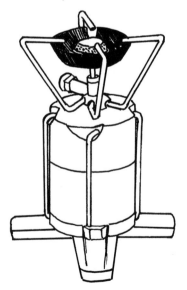

Fig. 12. Bleuet (butane) stove is light and is easy to operate, but less efficient than kerosene or gasoline stove in very cold weather.

1. British Thermal Unit, which expresses the heat value of various fuels. One formula describes a BTU as the heat required to raise the temperature of one pound of water one degree Fahrenheit, starting at 39 degrees.

lent stoves designed to burn it. However, since it is less volatile, a kerosene stove must be primed or preheated in order to ignite the kerosene. This often means carrying two fuels. Also, kerosene is somewhat malodorous and spillage on clothing or equipment produces a smell that remains for days.

Gasoline seems to be the best choice. It is available almost anywhere in the world and is highly volatile (hence, lights easily even in extremely cold weather); its odor dissipates quickly, and even following the sharp price increases of 1974, it is still much less expensive than either butane or propane. And safe containers for its transportation in bulk are available.

White gasoline, or one of the specially refined fuels designed for use in gasoline stoves[2], is preferable. White gas contains no lead (tetra-ethyl) added to automotive gasolines as an anti-knock compound. It is not true, however, that automotive, or leaded gasoline, cannot be burned in backpackers' stoves. The additives tend to clog the needle

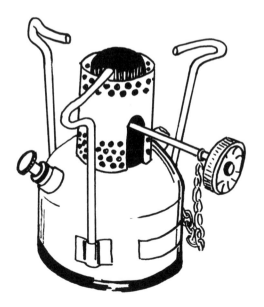

Fig. 13. Phoebus Model 625 (gasoline) stove provides hot flame and features tank with large capacity. This type of stove performs very well at high altitude.

---

2. Coleman fuel, for example, is naphtha especially adapted to camp-stove and lantern use. Its only drawbacks are its greater-than-gasoline cost and the susceptibility of its containers to damage under rough handling by packers. Otherwise, it is a very efficient and clean liquid fuel.

valve and orifice sooner than if white gas is used exclusively, and noxious fumes are more noticeable, but stoves will operate quite well. What's more, leaded gas is much more easily obtainable than the unleaded type, especially in more remote areas.

Precautions should be observed, whether you use naphtha, white or leaded gasoline. Ventilation should always be provided as a safeguard against carbon monoxide or, in a small tent, against the loss of oxygen. In a fabric shelter, the latter may not be severe, but enough to cause nausea or a headache. All in all, however, gasoline or naphtha is the best choice.

Comparison of Heat Values

Fuel	Heat Value Per Gallon
Kerosene	132,500 BTU's
Naphtha	121,000 BTU's
Gasoline	119,200 BTU's
Butane	101,000 BTU's
Propane	91,800 BTU's
Alcohol (Methyl)	64,400 BTU's

A mountain stove must be rugged—backpacking is not a gentle form of transportation, especially under difficult conditions. The stove must also be stable. A pot of hot soup spilled into the snow at the end of an arduous day is

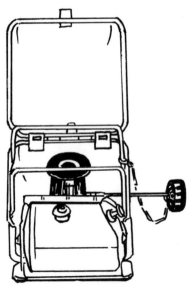

Fig. 14. Optimus Model 111 (kerosene) or 111-B (gasoline) has pressure pump built into carrying case. This type is excellent in cold weather and provides stable base for cooking pot.

no laughing matter. Most important, though, the stove should be equipped with a pressure pump. Pumping eliminates the need for priming, a messy, time-consuming procedure wherein the tank must be warmed with the bare hands, or fuel must be splashed on the burner head and lighted. Once hot enough to vaporize, the fuel then burns. A pump does away with all of this. Pressure is built up, a opened, and a lighted match applied. You're ready to cook.

A smoky, yellow flame means that the burner is not yet hot enough; the tank is almost empty, or has been overfilled. Possibly there is not enough oxygen to support combustion. Lighting procedures vary slightly from stove to stove, and directions should be followed faithfully. Always clean a stove when you return from a trip; then test it thoroughly before departing on another. Spare parts should be carried, those most apt to need replacing being the nipple, pump washer, and tank gasket. If your stove requires separate needles for cleaning the orifice, carry several since they're easily damaged or lost. Some stoves have a built-in cleaning needle but even these must be replaced occasionally.

Two types of burners are available, a "silent" burner, with numerous tiny holes on a hemispherical head, each hole producing a tiny, separate flame. Some consider these more efficient, and certainly their lack of noise is an advantage if used inside a tent. The other style is the "roarer" burner, which works—and sounds—like a small blowtorch. This type has a single flame ring which, once heated, ignites fuel vapor as it rushes by. While noisy, this burner is usually windproof to a degree.

Bad weather or extreme cold can often make cooking inside the tent necessary, and this is always a little risky. Care must be taken not to allow the stove to overheat, possibly rupturing the tank or popping the safety valve, thus spewing gasoline vapor and triggering an explosion. Lacking a "cook hole" in the tent floor, carry an asbestos pad on which to place the stove. This protects the floor fabric, and prevents snow under the floor from melting, and possibly tilting the stove. Such pads are available at most hardware stores.

PRESSURE COOKERS

Cooking in cold weather and/or at high altitudes presents two major problems. Cold air quickly draws heat away from aluminum cookware, thus increasing cooking time and fuel consumption. Also, at high altitudes, water boils at a relatively low temperature due to reduced air pressure. Since food can be heated only to the temperature at which water boils—and this may be only 185 to 190 degrees Farenheit—you may have to carry 50 percent more fuel than would be needed at low altitudes.

Fig. 15. Pressure cooker like this 5¼-quart type saves time and fuel in cold weather or at high altitude.

A pressure cooker offsets this loss in cooking efficiency since it is not affected by decreased atmospheric pressure. Its extra weight is usually far less than that of extra fuel necessary when cooking with conventional pots. And cooking time is speeded up phenomenally.

VACUUM BOTTLES

If uninsulated, hot soups and drinks cool rapidly in cold weather. However, vacuum bottles can make these available at anytime on the trail where they can be sipped leisurely. Not only are hot liquids comforting but they are also essential in the treatment of hypothermia. A good trick is to make a hot soup at breakfast, or just before breaking camp, then seal it in a vacuum bottle. You can then enjoy hot soup for lunch or that evening while the main course is being prepared. There's an infinite variety of freeze-dried soups suitable for this use, along with hot chocolate and Ovaltine.

FLASHLIGHT

A headlamp is more practical than a hand-held flashlight since it frees the hands for more essential work. Also, batteries—which deteriorate rapidly when cold—can be carried inside the clothing for warmth. Extra bulbs can be taped inside the reflector. Low-intensity bulbs create less drain on the batteries although the light is less bright. A higher-amperage bulb, in case brighter light is necessary, should also be carried, along with spare batteries. Practice changing these in the dark. You may have to do it on an exposed ridge in a howling storm some night. That's when practice pays off.

COMPASS

Navigating in the mountains often requires a compass. Known landmarks have a habit of hiding behind the clouds when you need them. A mountaineer's compass need not be elaborate but it should be a sturdy one which includes an azimuth scale instead of the almost useless N, E, S, and W quadrant points on cheap compasses. The Silva compasses are clearly marked for day or night travel and incorporate a direction-of-travel indicator when plotting your course from a map. More sophisticated compasses include a sighting device which increases accuracy when taking a bearing. The best advice about a compass is: Don't wait until you need it desperately to figure out how it works! That will be too late.

KNIFE

Only a tenderfoot carries a large sheath knife hanging at his belt. Swiss army-type knives, available in several models, are much more practical since they include a variety of necessary tools in addition to one or two blades. Look for one that has a Phillips screwdriver, for example. Using this, you can tinker with ski bindings, camera equipment, or portable radios. Some of these knives include a tiny but handy saw.

WATCH

Unless you want to risk losing or damaging the watch you ordinarily wear, carry one of the many cheap but remarkably reliable watches now on the market. You may not have any appointments to keep in the mountains, but it's good to know how much daylight you have left during which to locate a suitable campsite. A watch also helps you gauge your progress. And it's comforting to awaken at 4 a.m. to note that you still have two hours to sleep!

CANTEEN

Drinking water is not always at hand when you want it. It's noble to bear the thirst bravely, and it's also foolish, especially at high altitude. Here, dehydration is a dangerous possibility. Carry a canteen; drink from it reasonably whenever the urge strikes. I prefer polyethylene bottles to metal canteens, not only because they are lighter and less expensive, but also because aluminum sometimes reacts to certain chemicals in water, imparting an unpleasant taste or even creating slightly poisonous compounds.

SUNGLASSES OR GOGGLES

The intensity of sunlight in the thin air of high altitude, particularly with snow on the ground, can result in serious eye discomfort or even permanent damage. Light reflected off the snow can cause injury. Generally speaking, the higher the altitude, the darker the glasses should be. If you normally wear eyeglasses, consider prescription sun goggles. Otherwise buy the very best you can find, among the regular dark glasses. It may be difficult to find snowproof glasses (the type worn by alpine skiers) that will fit over prescription lenses. You may have to modify either. *And if you're off to the mountains for an extended period, carry an extra pair of prescription and sun goggles.*

CAMERA AND FILM

Take lots of pictures. An extension arm on the focusing ring will facilitate picture-taking and encourage greater use of your camera, even when it's too cold to remove your gloves or mittens. Always take more film than you think you'll need.

PARACHUTE CORD

Just as no woodsman goes into the forest without a length of rope, no mountaineer should be without a hank (at least 50 feet long) of ⅛-inch nylon parachute cord. It will tuck almost anywhere in a pack and will have dozens of uses—replacing broken boot laces, tying splints into place, or lashing skis together to form a toboggan.

Living in the mountains as I do, I'm occasionally called out to join search and rescue parties, so I keep a ready-to-go, fully assembled pack of all the foregoing gear at hand. Then, I don't have to rummage about at the last minute, with the possibility of overlooking a critical bit of equipment. In addition, there's a first-aid kit without which I never go into the mountains.

FIRST-AID KIT

This should include the following items in sufficient quantity to serve a moderate-size party, yet it should be light enough for one man to carry on a day climb.

1. Adhesive bandages (25 assorted)
2. Adhesive tape (1 small roll)
3. Sterile gauze compresses (2, medium size)
4. Clean triangular bandage (in plastic bag)
5. Aspirin or other pain-relieving compound
6. Waterproof matches
7. Small pair of scissors
8. Antiseptic ointment
9. Moleskin (about 10 square inches)
10. Elastic bandages (3 inches wide with clip)
11. Four or five large safety pins
12. Burn ointment

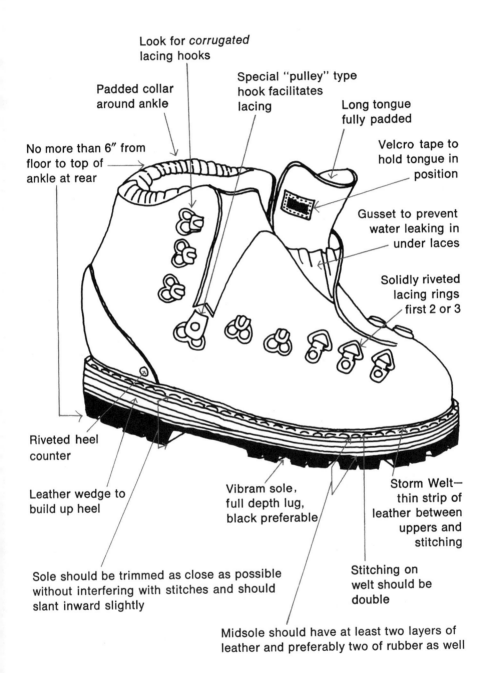

Look for *corrugated* lacing hooks

Padded collar around ankle

Special "pulley" type hook facilitates lacing

Long tongue fully padded

No more than 6″ from floor to top of ankle at rear

Velcro tape to hold tongue in position

Gusset to prevent water leaking in under laces

Solidly riveted lacing rings first 2 or 3

Riveted heel counter

Leather wedge to build up heel

Vibram sole, full depth lug, black preferable

Storm Welt— thin strip of leather between uppers and stitching

Sole should be trimmed as close as possible without interfering with stitches and should slant inward slightly

Stitching on welt should be double

Midsole should have at least two layers of leather and preferably two of rubber as well

Fig. 16. Drawing shows desirable features to look for when buying medium-weight hiking and climbing boot

chapter 8
Specialized Climbing Footwear

No single type of mountaineering footwear is suitable, or even safe, for every condition. There is no such thing as an "all-round" boot. Some climbers, in fact, own four, five, or even more pairs of climbing shoes, each geared to different seasons and situations.

Furthermore, boot materials and workmanship vary tremendously. A small fraction of today's boots are of superior quality, will last for years and increase the pleasure of climbing, their fit actually improving with use. Such boots are expensive. Others range from mediocre (good for a few seasons, at best) to miserable, virtually guaranteed to disintegrate under hard use. Buy the best boot you can afford! Beginners sometimes ignore this maxim and seek a bargain, possibly hoping to buy other gear with the "savings." Back off from this temptation.

Quality is not always easy to recognize, so here are some buying tips. Brand names may mean little. Several well-known bootmakers, in order to broaden their market, produce shoddy, bottom-of-the-line boots along with their better models. Too often a bootmaker's good reputation is based on a single style of boot, excellent for a specialized purpose, while his other production is inferior. Occasionally, too, boots without a label or trademark are sold in boxes bearing the name of a famed maker. These are probably seconds or the product of an obscure outfit. The quality of an unlabeled boot is suspect.

Some otherwise reputable manufacturers mass-produce a mediocre or inferior boot to be sold under a different label by so-called discount houses and high-volume

Steele Glacier Expedition approaches Yukon's Gibson Glacier, where rocky rubble demands high-quality boots.

retail outlets. These may be advertised as "boots by a famous maker," or "made to our exacting specifications." This is usually gobbledegook. A good boot invariably bears the label of its *maker*, not that of a retailer.

The maker of a superb boot has been known to downgrade quality through the use of inferior materials and shortcuts in manufacturing, riding on his good reputation. This downgrading is usually gradual, difficult to detect. Spotting shortcomings in boot quality isn't, therefore, easy to do, but there are ways.

First, there's the type and quality of leather. Is it "full-grain" or "split," chrome-tanned, oil- or vegetable-tanned? Ask the salesman. Too often, he neither knows nor appreciates the difference. "Full-grain" refers to leather cut from the full thickness of a hide after it has been defleshed and the hair removed. This is usually too thick for dress or street shoes, so it is split into sheets of varying thicknesses. The outermost layer may go into such items as wallets or hand luggage, while the remainder may be used for utility shoes, boots, or straps. The thinner "top-grain" or "upper split" provides a light, supple leather for street shoes and light hiking boots.

Climbing boots, however, require greater thickness for strength, durability, and support. This calls for "full-grain," unsplit leather. Especially in a lightweight boot, don't be misled by a seemingly natural "grain" or outer surface. It may be split cowhide with an artificially produced grain!

The outermost layers of hide are more compact and the pores smaller, allowing it to "breathe" while providing greater water-repellency than the more porous under-layers. This is one vital reason why "top" or "full-grain" leathers are preferable to "bottom-grain" or "splits." Split-grain leather can be artificially compacted by heat and pressure and this increases water-repellency, but it also decreases suppleness and "breathability," both of which are obviously desirable.

Very well, you want boots that breathe and are comfortably supple (while providing adequate support), yet you don't want them to leak. Some very good boots are advertised as waterproof. The manufacturers can be forgiven for the claim, since the more expensive "waterproof" types made today have sealed seams and the leather is impregnated with a silicone compound. They do keep out water effectively for some time, and the effectiveness can be renewed by applying one of the commercial dressings later on. Regardless of claims, however, the application will have to be repeated periodically.

"Active" leather (and what is more active than shoe leather on a hike or during a climb?) cannot be truly waterproofed. It can only be made water-repellent. Only rubber or plastic boots are fully impervious to moisture, but these materials also hamper the outward passage of moisture from inside the boots. Any type of dressing applied to porous leather to "waterproof" it, may do so temporarily by sealing the pores. But it does not last.

Because smooth-finished top-grain leather is easily scuffed, even cut partway through in hard usage—thus opening the way for moisture to enter—some bootmakers reverse the full grain in the uppers. This retains the advantage of the more compact "top grain" but this is then on the inside, termed "reverse grain." This protects the top grain from abrasion and scuffing, of course, but it also makes it difficult to apply a water-repellency solution to the more porous "split," now on the outside.

Oil- and vegetable-tanned leathers are inherently more water-repellent than chrome-tanned leathers, and considerably more expensive. Processing time for the latter is short and it produces a soft, pliable leather not suitable for hard use.

Suede finishes are popular on lightweight hiking boots, on technical-climbing shoes, or on Klettershoes (described below). However, suedes cannot be treated with a water-repelling solution without ruining their appearance. Suede does resist scuffing well, though. This type of boot, for light hiking and climbing, should be kept dry and cleaned with a soft wire brush.

TYPES OF CLIMBING BOOTS

The most highly specialized boot designed exclusively for climbing is the Klettershoe (or *Klettershue*, to use the original German spelling), a lightweight rock-climbing shoe. It looks like a high-topped basketball sneaker except that the uppers are of suede leather. Some European models have a non-stretch canvas upper but these may wear fairly quickly, being quite susceptible to abrasion.

While made primarily for rock climbing, Klettershoes are adaptable to light hiking but they offer little ankle support or protection from rock bruises. Nor are they water-repellent. In fact, because of the materials and glues used in their making, they will not withstand wetting without damage. Keep them dry! A snug fit is important, too, though not so snug that they are uncomfortable.

This snug fit, and the lightness of Klettershoes, allow a climber to maintain an intimate and sensitive contact with rock surfaces, required for precise footing and delicate movement on a precarious slope. The lightness of the shoe also adds to the feeling of freedom and grace essential to the enjoyment of climbing.

Klettershoes have a thin lug sole, usually half the thickness of the Vibram sole found on heavier climbing boots. No particular version of the many patterns of lugs seems to offer a distinct advantage. More important is the quality and consistency of the rubber. If it is too soft the lugs will crumble prematurely and provide a poor grip on varying rock surfaces. If, on the other hand, the rubber is too hard, the lugs fail to "give" sufficiently to grip well on small crystals and will prove very slippery on wet or damp rock. A sole of medium hardness is best for both wear and grip. You can recognize a suitable sole simply by pressing a fingernail into it. A permanent impression in the rubber should result but you should not be able to deform one of the lugs with mere finger pressure.

Even color will help you in your appraisal. Rubber or composition soles of any color but black are invariably too soft, especially those in brown or yellow, and those which are clear or untinted. Eventually any sole will wear, of course, but a good pair of Klettershoes can always be resoled.

There are at least 14 styles of Klettershoes, but only two have any special advantages for certain types of climbing. The first is the smooth-soled Klettershoe. This has no lugs and no hollow in the instep, thus providing a larger gripping surface for friction climbing on smooth, glacially polished slabs. But on coarse rock surfaces, where small bumps and crystals exist, the Vibram lug sole grips more securely. Smooth soles are extremely treacherous on patches of lichen or grass, which are frequently present on the higher and less-travelled cliffs. On wet rock, too, smooth soles are a definite hazard. Even lug soles don't provide the traction here that the old hobnailed boots did, but they are less prone to slip than a smooth sole since they do not depend solely on friction. A film of water, or even the humidity of a warm summer day can make friction climbing on smooth slabs virtually impossible, no matter what type of sole is on your boot.

At high camp on Tocllaraju, Cordillera Blanca, Peru,
proper boots, tent, packs, clothing, and gear assure comfort.

The second major variation of the Klettershoe is the "RR", which was designed by Royal Robbins for special conditions found in California's Yosemite Valley but has since become almost universally adopted by serious technical climbers throughout the United States. However, being a compromise between a very light, flexible Klettershoe and a heavier climbing boot, it may not be the optimum climbing shoe for every situation. But it does have distinct advantages. For example, it features a continuous strip of rubber, about one inch high, all around the foot extending upward from the sole, and this is very helpful in situations where the foot is jammed into vertical cracks. The rubber strip provides a firm grip, much better than is possible with leather or canvas. The "RR" has a steel shank that imparts a degree of lateral stiffness, allowing the boot to "edge" more efficiently on small crystals and flakes. In addition, there is a special lacing arrangement that allows the toe to be loosened or tightened independently of the heel and instep. This, combined with its heavier weight, makes it possible to hike short distances to and from cliff areas without the need for changing into and out of hiking boots. The shoe's added weight, however, detracts from the sensitivity and lightness so desirable in a purely technical rock-climbing shoe.

Next to consider is the medium-weight hiking and climbing boot, with a full-thickness Vibram sole, heavy construction throughout, and normally padded on the inside to cushion and protect the feet.

The Vibram sole should be stitched or screwed to the boot through the midsole. Gluing or vulcanizing is not adequate. Look for at least one layer of rubber and one of leather, preferably two of each, in the midsole. These are usually stitched to the uppers and the lug sole is then screwed and glued to these. Check carefully that no nails or screws penetrate into the boot. The thicker the midsole, the warmer the boot will be, since most heat is lost by conduction into the ground. The fewer pieces of leather in the uppers, the fewer will be the seams to part and leak. The tongue should be long and padded, and connected to the uppers by a gusset on either side, or there should be a separate gusset forward of the tongue.

This helps keep out water and dirt. Padding should be adequate to result in a fairly close fit, but not so snug that movement of heel and calf tendons is impaired. For this reason, climbing boots should be no more than five or six inches high. Even where the top two inches of an eight-inch boot comprise a foam-filled collar, such boots will

Rappeling climber is wearing gaiters, which keep snow and scree out of comfortably low boots.

prove overly restrictive. At any rate, don't rely on elastic collars to keep snow or scree (loose talus pebbles, dirt, and other debris) out of your boots. Use gaiters instead. Too high a boot will chafe your lower calf and shin, particularly when traveling downhill. Wear boots that are cut down slightly at the back. During technical ice climbing, or when walking some distance on moderately angled rock slabs, this permits greater foot freedom.

With the exception of the heel counter, all seams in the uppers (if any) should face or overlap to the rear so that they can't catch easily and tear out. Ideally, heel counters should be riveted at the lower forward corners. Note carefully whether the lacing hooks and rings are well set and, at least on heavier boots, these should be of the two-rivet type. Such rivets should not be exposed on the inside, but covered by the interior leather lining; otherwise chafing and outward heat conduction will result. Corrugated hooks are much stronger than smooth ones. I prefer two or three lacing rings near the toe and strong hooks above these. In better-quality boots, the tongue will be held in closed position by a short piece of Velcro tape. For medium to heavy boots, suede uppers are definitely not as desirable as rough-out, or smooth, full-grain leathers.

The heaviest of all, of course, are the double boots worn by high-altitude climbers or technical climbers under winter conditions. With certain exceptions, everything true about medium or heavy boots also applies to double boots. The inner boot is normally of felt covered with leather. Sometimes the latter can be removed from the felt which can then be changed like socks, obviously an advantage when moisture is a problem. In very cold weather, however, this is probably of marginal value. On the other hand, inner boots of one-piece felt with leather permanently attached often fit better and are more carefully made. For delicate climbing on mixed terrain in cold weather, a good fit will give you a better feel for the rock underneath, although at best, double boots are relatively clumsy. The sole of the inner boot should be of thin, knurled or "sandpaper" rubber, so that you can walk outside for a few moments wearing only your inner boots. This type of sole will keep them dry and prevent slipping.

Naturally, the outer boot should be of the best possible quality, with double-riveted lacing rings, full-gusseted tongue, and a Vibram lug sole. It's often made with a square toe and a cable groove to permit the use of the old-fashioned "bear trap" ski bindings, which are often utilized on ski mountaineering expeditions.

Double boots are nearly always at least 10 inches high, but because they do not fit unduly tightly, this should pose no problems. In trying on a pair, however, lean far forward to flex your ankles. There should be no chafing on the shinbone. In many such boots, a fold of leather halfway up the heel acts as a hinge to facilitate this flexing.

Don't delude yourself that boots which do not fit when new will fit later on! The notion that they will mold to your feet after a few days of hiking is untrue in most instances. Since your feet constantly change shape as you walk, and swell somewhat during the day, boots are obviously not going to develop a glove-like fit if that fit is bad to start with. Satisfy yourself that the boots are right for you. Don't accept a salesman's word. Check these points:

1. The boots must be long enough. Walk about in them, scuffing your feet, striking the toes against a hard object such as a wall baseboard. If your toes more than barely touch up forward, the boots are too short. Boots may stretch in width but never in length.

2. The heel must fit snugly but not so tightly that it binds.

3. The arch should be right for your feet. If you have problems with your arches, boots can generally be built up or even hammered down in the instep, but try to get them right to start with. Improvisations may not work perfectly. Most Americans have much wider feet than the French or Italians, and consequently boots made in France or Italy may prove too narrow. German and Swiss boots tend to be wider with low arches.

Naturally, you should wear appropriate socks when trying on boots, or while being measured for a custom-made pair. In any case, boots made specifically for you are the best choice. But if you must confine yourself to ready-made footwear, shop carefully. At times, you may not be able to obtain a good fit from among boots stocked by a particular retailer. Look elsewhere then. Boots are one of your most important investments. Proper selection and fit are vital.

*Conducting high-altitude research for Arctic Institute,
climbers dress to cope with rigors of Mount Logan.*

Clothing serves much the same functions for the mountaineer as for anyone else. It provides warmth and shields him against rain, snow, and wind. However, a climber's clothes must also protect him against minor bumps and abrasions handed out by rough rock, crusty snow, and ice.

Several layers of light clothing are, in general, more comfortable and warmer than a single heavy layer. Clothes do not produce heat but, like a sleeping bag, trap air in their fibers and in between their layers to produce an insulating dead-air space that retards heat loss. Several layers are more adaptable to rapidly changing conditions and varying temperatures. It is important to avoid sweating during the winter, and at high altitudes in the summer,

In warmth of mid-morning, climber wears comfortable turtleneck shirt, having peeled off jacket and sweater.

since this wets the clothing, vastly decreasing its insulating value. With several layers of light clothing, it is easy to compensate for changing conditions; simply remove a layer if you're too warm, add one if chilled.

Only when numerous layers might prove too cumbersome or excessively heavy should you opt for a bulkier single layer. For instance, three sweaters which might result in a restrictive fit, hampering the use of arms and shoulders, would be a poorer choice than a single down jacket. But, on the whole, the principle of layering is sound.

Old but sturdy clothes of almost any description are suitable for rock climbing if the weather is mild, but cold weather, high altitudes, and the possibility of storms dictate a careful selection among castoffs. Check every detail, even shoelaces!

Inspect carefully any garment that is to be modified for climbing to be sure that it is truly serviceable. Pants, jackets, and other items should be liberally reinforced in critical places—particularly the seat and the elbows; buttons and buttonholes need reinforcement, too. Any type of fastener—zipper, snap, button, or lacing—should be tested with an eye to replacement if necessary.

Be even more critical of new clothing since, after all, you're laying out new dollars for it. Look especially for full-cut designs in shirts, sweaters, pants, and parkas as a guarantee of unrestricted arm and leg movement. It's tough enough plodding through deep snow without the handicap of restrictive garments. Turtleneck sweaters and shirts to be worn tucked into the trousers should be long enough to stay there, not to gap when you bend over. Parkas must hang down freely over the buttocks.

Every detail should be inspected, so that once you've made a choice you can reasonably expect several seasons of dependable service.

UNDERWEAR

Wool is, without question, the warmest of all fabrics, even when damp or wet. Some, however, find that wool next to the skin is "itchy," and for such persons there are wool-cotton combinations. Itchiness contributes nothing to warmth, after all, so there's no reason to tolerate it. Warmth is a function of thickness and insulating dead-air space, which can be achieved by combining the wool with something that doesn't itch. Nylon underwear, on the other hand, has no place in mountaineering—not even one-piece leotards since nylon is an ineffective insulation and it does not "wick" perspiration away from the body as do wool and cotton. The latter draw dampness away from the skin to the outer layers of clothing where there is enough air to evaporate it. This provides a feeling of warmth.

Fishnet-type underwear provides the best ventilation. During the summer, this is worn in a single layer under a loose-fitting shirt and trousers, but in the winter an additional layer over fishnet fabric must be worn for maximum insulation. However, I find that a single layer of wool-cotton mixture is the most comfortable, least restrictive, and warmest. Cut your long underwear off just below the knees! This frees the calves for full freedom in walking or climbing without noticeable heat drain from the legs.

For extremely cold conditions the fluffy Norwegian underwear is hard to beat, but it's difficult to find in the United States except possibly in shops handling marine clothing. It was designed for winter wear by Norwegian fishermen in the North Sea.

SOCKS

Each of us must experiment with socks to find the right type and combination. Wool, of course, is the only basic material that is practical, since as pointed out, it remains relatively warm even when wet. Also, it does not compress easily and is durable. Some wool socks are reinforced with nylon at the toe and heel; this is an excellent feature, as it makes the socks even sturdier.

One pair of medium to heavy socks is always preferable to combinations of light- to heavyweight footwear. This makes sense. Your foot will better fit your boot if there is only a single layer between skin and leather. Insulation results from dead-air space, not from compacted layers of fibers. If the boot is sufficiently large—and it must be to be warm—one pair of socks will allow more foot freedom and more air around the foot. Several pairs of socks tend to squeeze the foot and eliminate this air space, resulting in cold feet.

If you can't stand the feel of wool, a very thin pair of cotton or silk inner socks will not materially depreciate the effectiveness of the wool. However, when socks are worn one pair over another, the sizes should be graduated upward. If two pairs of the same size are worn, the inner socks are apt to wrinkle or bunch up, promoting chafing and blisters.

PANTS AND KNICKERS

Pants and knickers should be of a closely woven, long-wearing, and abrasion-resistant material. Various types of wool and Orlon whipcord possess these characteristics. But other details of design and construction are to be considered.

A zipper fly is less troublesome than buttons but must be equipped with a self-locking slider. All pockets must have flaps which can be fastened with buttons, snaps, or Velcro tape to exclude snow. Belt loops need to be rugged, preferably of the tunnel type. Heavy pants for winter climbing may be more comfortably and efficiently held up by suspenders than by a belt. Buttons at the appropriate points around the waist must be securely attached. A double seat and reinforced crotch are desirable, as are double knees and a double front on the legs above the knees.

Knickers allow greater freedom of movement than trousers, especially in the knees. Pants, unless cut full, often interfere with acrobatic rock climbing. Various types of fasteners close the legs of knickers but lacings or Velcro tape are definitely superior to buckle-type fastenings, since the latter easily catch on protruding rocks and overhanging brush, sometimes being pulled off.

Surplus wool serge uniform trousers can be converted to satisfactory climbing pants or knickers if they are reinforced in the crotch, seat, and knees. When buying these, select a pair with extra-long legs. When the legs are cut to size—especially if they are cut for knickers—you'll have ample extra material for patches and reinforcing.

SHIRTS AND SWEATERS

Unless well-cut and of good quality, the body of a turtleneck shirt or sweater is likely to be skimpy—not long enough or wide enough through the shoulders for unrestricted movement. Tails that pull out expose the skin to cold air and snow, a potentially dangerous situation. Light- or medium weight wool shirts are a good choice, provided the tails are ample. Even when wet or damp, they provide warmth. Don't hesitate to have a shirt altered for a perfect fit. A slight modification of sleeve length or body width may increase the garment's usefulness and comfort.

JACKETS AND ANORAKS

These are primarily windbreakers whose function is to enhance the insulating values of the underlying layers. Here, too, the fit must be comfortable, with no arm or shoulder restriction.

Atop Wyoming's Grand Teton, Tom Lyman is pictured in windbreaking jacket that permits freedom of movement.

There is no need to define a jacket, of course, but the *anorak* probably needs explaining. It's basically a parka of the pullover type, without zipper or snaps on the front, and it reaches almost to the knees. It may be provided with a strap passing between the legs and joining the front and back to hold the garment close to the body and to keep it from ballooning in the wind. Its hood must be large enough to fit over a balaclava or "heavy hat," and designed to turn with the head. Otherwise, the entire upper body may have to be turned to afford a view to either side, an impossible movement in some climbing situations. A tunnel, perhaps 1½ inches wide, around the face opening of the hood will deflect some of the wind. The hood should also be equipped with a drawstring closure, a necessity in severe weather. Some sort of a locking device on the drawstring is required, too, since it's virtually impossible to tie this in a conventional knot while wearing mittens.

On the whole, however, jackets are preferable to anoraks. They are easier to ventilate and more adaptable to varying conditions. Be sure that the zipper is backed up by snaps, thus guaranteeing that the jacket can be closed snugly even if the zipper ices or malfunctions. The zipper should also be provided with a second slider, at the bottom, so that this can be opened for ventilation even while the jacket remains closed at the throat. Patch pockets are handy for sunglasses, candy, film, and other small items, but without securely closed flaps they will fill with snow. Wrists should be sealed against wind and snow, Velcro tape being excellent for snuggling the sleeve cuffs. Perhaps the most popular material for jackets and wind shells is 60/40 cloth, a durable fabric made of 60 percent cotton and 40 percent nylon.

FOUL-WEATHER GEAR

Foul-weather gear must keep you dry, of course, but to be fully effective in mountaineering it must also be loose-fitting, as light as possible, and durable. Waterproofed nylon comes close to this, being lighter than most rubberized fabrics though not quite as sturdy.

A poncho is the simplest form of rainwear but it's difficult to manage in a high wind and it makes rope work virtually impossible. A better choice is the two-piece suit— pants and jacket. The latter can double as a windbreaker during the summer and the pants are suitable for that purpose in the winter. However, since waterproof fabrics do not breathe, excessive condensation can occur, thus wetting the inner clothing. For this reason the jacket must be well vented under the arms, and the pants ventilated in the legs. The lightweight, two-piece suit is at its best in the summer. For winter conditions, I prefer a jacket of 60/40 cloth as a windbreaker and storm jacket.

HATS AND BALACLAVAS

Going bareheaded can account for up to 45 percent of your body's heat loss in cold weather. This is foolhardy, so wear a hat. Wool is warmest, though climbers prefer less-irritating Orlon. *Balaclavas* are knitted toques which can be rolled down over the entire head, the front forming a face mask with openings for eyes, nose, and mouth. Even the latter two can be covered completely, though, leaving only the eyes exposed. In extreme weather, this eye opening can be protected with ski-type goggles to seal out cold and wind. Under certain conditions a skier's headband, designed to protect the ears alone, is helpful but it can never be a substitute for a full hat or balaclava.

MITTENS

Wool mittens are much warmer than any type of gloves. In very cold weather, mylar or silk gloves can be worn under these. Thus, the bulky mittens can be removed for a few moments at a time for picture-taking or other delicate chores without exposing the hands to quick frostbite. Several extra pairs of mittens should be carried during extended winter trips. Even on day hikes I always carry at least one extra set. Nylon or canvas shells over the mittens keep the latter dry, preserving their insulating capacity. *Idiot strings*—long cords or thongs which secure the mittens and shells to the jacket or parka sleeves, prevent loss or "blow away." Such strings are a nuisance, I'll grant, but the loss of mittens can lead to frostbite.

The most practical combination I've found consists of army-surplus leather-and-canvas shells worn over very closely knit Austrian wool mittens. The leather, though susceptible to wetting and stiffening, provides a firm grip on ice axes and hammers. Mittens and shells should be equipped with gauntlets to keep snow and cold from the wrists.

Climber rappels down Devil's tower in Wyoming. Rope is basic tool for technical descents as well as ascents.

chapter 10
Technical Climbing—
Rock and Rope

Most people begin their technical climbing (i.e., using ropes and pitons for protection or direct assistance) on sunny rock slopes and boulders far below the icy walls and cloud-wrapped spires of the higher peaks. It is well they do. While nearly every technique of rock climbing can be learned on a series of boulders barely a few feet off the ground, simply knowing how to make a move is not enough. Fingers that have no trouble gripping miniscule flakes on the side of a campground boulder have a disconcerting way of coming unstuck in similar situations when there is a 3,000-foot drop below the climber's feet, and the temperature hovers close to the freezing mark.

Climbing is both an art and a craft. The *craft* can be learned and practiced during a few afternoons, while the *art* of climbing can be mastered only after a long series of ascents on increasingly difficult stretches under varying conditions. Too often, a young climber can surmount a difficult problem on Tillie's Boulder with ridiculous ease but then finds himself and his party in serious trouble in a much easier situation, except that it's high on an exposed *arête*—a steep, sharp ridge—20 minutes before dark!

The craft of climbing can be outlined here, but the art cannot be learned or appreciated by reading a book. It evolves as a form of personal expression, as individual as the physical and mental traits of the climber himself. It involves judgment, the kind that comes from long experience and association with rock, wind, time, and distance, and it includes boldness based on supreme self-confidence and a sense of proportion. Occasionally, art becomes a calculated risk.

Craft, on the other hand, is knowledge, and skill in its application. Deft handling of the rope, the correct choice of nuts or pitons, the proper hold and grip for the type of crack or nubbin being climbed, efficiency in setting up belays and anchors—these are the elements of craft. Craft can substitute for art, though if it does a climber's style will suffer. However, art can never substitute for craft. The great artist knows his craft to a superlative degree and expresses himself through the skillful use of his tools as he relates to the medium of his expression. In climbing, artistic expression, style, and ethics all derive from a thorough appreciation for, and understanding of, the craft.

THE ROPE

The rope is the basic tool of climbing. Its limitations as well as its uses should be thoroughly understood. Virtually all serious climbers today use nylon rope of the *kernmantle*, or core-and-sheath, construction. This rope has better handling characteristics than laid rope, being softer and limper, and its smooth exterior surface creates less friction and resistance when sliding over rock or through carabiners. In addition, kernmantle rope has little tendency to spin when hanging freely from an overhang, thus facilitating jumaring and rappeling, especially where this is done on a single rope.

Rappeling is, of course, simply a controlled slide down an anchored rope, with the control achieved by friction through the hands and around the body or by means of a mechanical braking device. All such techniques, and the equipment involved, will be covered in detail in the appropriate sections of this book. Rappeling, for example, is treated in Chapter 12, which is devoted to rock-climbing techniques; and jumaring—an extremely important rope-climbing technique where crevasses are a danger—will come up again in Chapter 14, a discussion of glacier travel.

Using nylon kernmantle, Jennifer Lyman scales
Weissner Route of Cannon Mountain in New Hampshire.

Nonetheless, because it's better to be repetitious than unclear where safety is concerned, possibly unfamiliar terms are defined in the glossary and again in the text wherever necessary for clarity.

Jumaring, then, is ascending a hanging, fixed rope by means of two ratchet-like devices called jumars, one for each foot, which are attached to the rope when needed. Hanging from each jumar is a nylon sling about 5½ feet long. You put your feet into these loops, or stirrups, and use your hands to slide the jumars up the rope a bit at a time. Since they grip the climbing rope when weight is applied, they slide up but not down, enabling you to pull yourself out of a crevasse.

Modern climbing ropes are almost universally 150 feet in length (45.75 meters) and 7/16 inches (11mm.) in diam-

Rappeling steep rock on Peru's Cordillera Blanca, climbers take care to maintain solid belays.

eter. For certain big-wall climbs, or where belay stances are known to be more than 140 to 150 feet apart, ropes up to 180 feet long are occasionally employed. (Belaying, covered at length in Chapter 12, is the technique of anchoring yourself at a strategic point and then feeding out or taking in rope so that if another climber loses his hold you can stop his fall.) Ropes longer than 150 feet, however, are difficult to coil in the hand and are too heavy to be handled easily while packing or climbing. Kernmantle ropes are usually available in a wide range of colors which are helpful in identifying the running line, as opposed to static lines in complicated situations, or during complex rescue operations.

Ice climbing usually requires rope of the same length and diameter as that used for rock climbing, since a fall on ice can be as serious as one on steep rock, generating as much shock on the belayer and points of protection. What's more, a 7/16-inch is much easier to grip securely than a lighter rope, especially while wearing heavy gloves or mittens. For easy snow climbing or where the rope might be used only to stop a short slip rather than an actual fall, a ⅜-inch (9 mm.) rope might be preferable in order to eliminate several pounds of unnecessary weight. Even in these smaller diameters, the standard length remains 150 feet. All rope, whether braided, laid, or of the kernmantle type, smaller than ⅜-inch, is strictly for Prussic loops, hammer slings, threading nuts and similar purposes—*never* for climbing or rappels. The only exception is a 150-foot length of 5/16-inch line which may be carried as a *reepschnur*, or pull-down line for retrieving a rappel rope on a long series of full-length (150-foot) rappels. This saves weight, but such a rope is obviously inadequate for climbing. All ropes should be purchased new and be certified with the U.I.A.A.[1] label.

Available in many colors and widths, nylon webbing is extremely useful as waist loops, runners, hammer loops and *etriers* or stirrups for direct-aid climbing. (An etrier is

---

1. Union Internationale des Associations d'Alpinisme, which has established standards for mountaineering ropes under controlled test conditions.

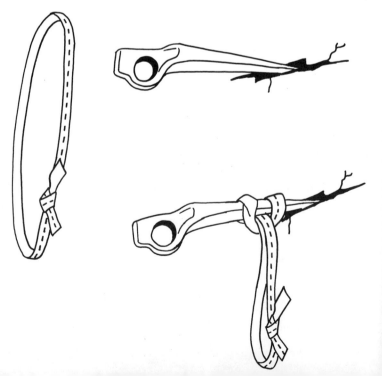

Fig. 17. Drawing at left shows etrier—*a set of three stirrups for direct-aid climbing—tied into inch-wide nylon webbing with carabiner attached.*

a set of three ladder-like steps made of webbing, for use where the rock offers no foothold. It is clipped by means of a carabiner to a piton or other anchor.) There are two types of nylon webbing—tubular which is rather soft and flexible, and solid flat which tends to be much stiffer. Both are quite strong, although only the full one-inch width, in either type, should be used where it might be expected to take the full weight of a hard fall. The stiffer webbing is more useful for etriers or stirrups, as the steps tend to stay

Fig. 18. Hero-loop is shown, below left, tied into ½-inch nylon webbing with water knot. Loop is about 12 inches long. Below, piton is shown in position in rock but driven in only partway. At bottom is hero-loop in place, looped over piton. It should be as close as possible to rock face to reduce leverage.

open, making it easier to insert the foot. Widths narrower than one inch are useful in direct-aid climbing for threading small nuts, manufacturing hammocks and belay seats, and making *hero-loops*. A hero-loop is a small (8- to 10-inch) nylon loop used to "tie off" a piton. Suppose you're using a four-inch piton and discover you can drive it only two inches into the rock. The piton's eye is at the outer end, and the farther it is from the rock the more leverage is exerted on it by the weight on a rope or etrier. Thus your anchor might pull out. To make sure it will hold, you reduce the leverage by wrapping a hero-loop around the exposed part of the piton—between the eye and the rock—and you can then clip an etrier to the loop, providing a foothold on which to work your way up. The hero-loop wraps around the piton and then through itself (Fig. 18).

Remember to use full-width webbing in all situations where it might have to check a long fall, or hold the weight of several climbers. Generally it is best to tie loops in webbing with the water knot or the grapevine knot (both of which are explained and illustrated later in this chapter, as are other recommended knots) rather than to sew them, as you may have to untie the loops in order to fasten several together. Sewn loops have demonstrated a wide variation in strength under tests. Ropes and webbing of materials other than nylon have no place in mountaineering.

A rope, of course, is of no use whatever until it is tied or hitched to an anchor point of some sort. The prime properties of rope are those of flexible connection, high tensile strength, and enough elasticity to absorb sudden stress. Chain or wire cable will also connect two points but with obvious disadvantages for climbers. A new 11mm. climbing rope has a rated tensile strength of approximately 5,800 pounds, actually somewhat more as this rated figure does not include a mandatory 20 percent safety margin. However, looping a rope around a bar of its own diameter, or less, reduces the rope's tensile strength by 50 percent. Tying a simple overhand knot in it will also reduce the strength by the same amount. This is because the individual fibers in the rope are stretched on the outside of a sharp curve and compressed on the inside. Under severe stress, strain is distributed among these fibers unevenly, so that, one by one, the fibers rupture. The rope breaks, or is damaged beyond further use. Some knots, such as the butterfly, eliminate bending the rope over small radii and consequently reduce the rope's strength by only 35 to 40 percent.

The most important property of a climbing rope, however, is not its high tensile strength but, rather, its elasticity and its related ability to absorb great destructive energy without breaking. This softens the shock transmitted to a climber or to the belayer in case of a hard fall. Incidentally, it also reduces the chance of breaking a piton or carabiner. Certain precautions must be observed, though:

1. Keep the rope clean. Never step on it, as this will grind in particles of grit. When the rope is later flexed, this grit will cut individual fibers and permanently weaken the rope. Combine this hidden damage with a 50 percent loss of strength when the line is looped through a carabiner or tied into a knot, and you may have little safety margin left. A 150-pound climber can easily generate more than 1,200 pounds of force during a hard fall!

2. Protect the rope from excessive heat, chemicals, gasoline, and oil, any of which can make nylon deteriorate quickly.

3. All climbing ropes should be stored in a cool, dry, *dark* place when not in use. Nylon is subject to deterioration by ultraviolet rays in sunlight. These won't hurt the fibers during the relatively short time actually spent in climbing, but beware of fixed ropes and rappel slings which have undergone several months of exposure to direct sunlight.

4. When a rope must be run over a sharp edge, round this edge with a hammer or pad it with a jacket, secured so that it won't be lost down the face. Each fiber in a nylon rope is thinner than a human hair and each contributes to strength, so minimize every cutting or abrasive influence.

5. Kinks in a climbing rope should be carefully and completely removed since they, too, distribute stress among the fibers unequally. Kinks can be removed by running the rope slowly through your closed hand as you walk along its length while the rope is stretched loosely on the ground, preferably in a grit-free area such as a lawn. Another method is to shake a rope up and down as it hangs freely, and full-length, from a cliff.

6. When not in use, keep the rope coiled in the simplest possible manner which is secure. You may need it in a hurry, and fancy chain or guide coils can only lead to grief while you struggle to uncoil the line.

KNOTS

During some 12 years of climbing, I doubt that I have used more than 10 or 12 different knots, some of these perhaps only once or twice in special situations. Assuming that you are working solely with nylon ropes of varying diameters, and with flat or tubular nylon webbing, certain knots are more efficient than others. Nylon has two distinct properties affecting knots. First, it is slippery. Second, because it stretches, a nylon line under stress will shrink in diameter, drawing up a knot very tightly. Then, when tension is released, the diameter reverts to somewhat near its original thickness. The knot then "freezes" in the line and becomes practically impossible to untie.

Most climbers have favorite knots, usually those to which they were first introduced, and some of these may not be entirely suitable! Some knots are strong and will hold well under varying loads but when the rope becomes wet or icy, become impossible to untie. A mountaineer's knot, however, must be such that it can be untied easily and quickly. Based on these considerations, on actual tests of tensile strength, and on practicality under field conditions, I recommend the following knots. These will be found adequate for all but a few special situations likely to be encountered only during rescue work or rock engineering on big walls.

Recommended Knots and Applications
(In the Climbing Rope)

1. Bowline on a Coil. (Fig. 19) The best knot for tying directly into the end of a climbing rope, as is usually done for drop-rope climbing; or in the event that you have lost all of your gear and have nothing left to work with but your rope.

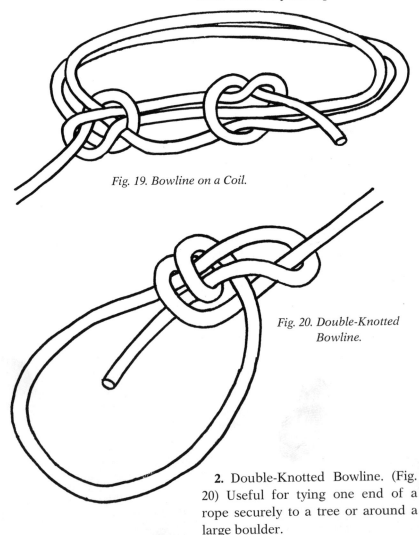

Fig. 19. Bowline on a Coil.

Fig. 20. Double-Knotted Bowline.

2. Double-Knotted Bowline. (Fig. 20) Useful for tying one end of a rope securely to a tree or around a large boulder.

3. Bowline on a Bight. (Fig. 21) Perhaps the most difficult knot to tie correctly time after time. It is extremely useful as a middleman's knot, and for rigging a self-equalizing anchor for belaying or lowering.

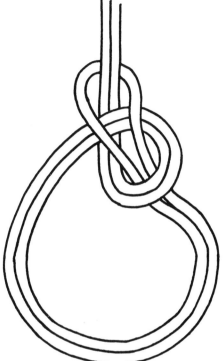

Fig. 21. Bowline on a Bight.

Fig. 22. Double-Knotted Sheet Bend.

4. Double-Knotted Sheet Bend. (Fig. 22) The *only* knot to use when tying two ropes together for a rappel, especially good when the ropes are of different diameters.

5. Figure-Eight Knot. (Fig. 23) A stopper knot to prevent an end from slipping through a pulley or Prussick. This should be tied on all rappels before the ropes are thrown down the face.

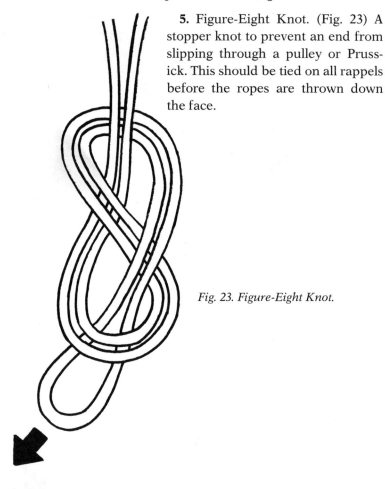

Fig. 23. Figure-Eight Knot.

Fig. 24. Double Fisherman's Knot.

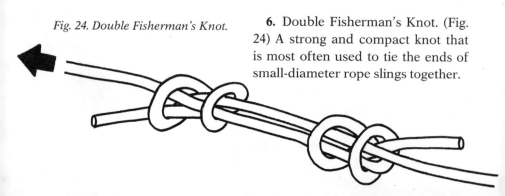

6. Double Fisherman's Knot. (Fig. 24) A strong and compact knot that is most often used to tie the ends of small-diameter rope slings together.

7. Butterfly Knot. (Fig. 25) I prefer this to all other loop knots. It is simple to tie and reduces the rope's strength by only 35 to 40 percent. Also, it can always be untied, even when the ropes are wet or icy. Used occasionally when a loop is clipped into a carabiner to anchor a line.

Fig. 25. Butterfly Knot.

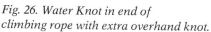

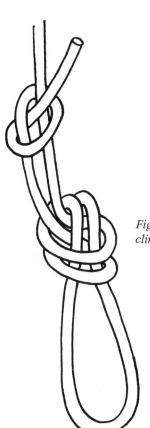

Fig. 26. Water Knot in end of climbing rope with extra overhand knot.

8. Water Knot. (Fig. 26) Basically an overhand loop tied into the end of the rope and used to secure the climbing rope to the waist or harness. Simple, compact, and sturdy, it gets tighter as stress is applied.

9. Prussick Knot. (Fig. 27) This is really a type of hitch which can be used either while climbing up a vertically hanging rope, or to seize and secure a running line. Normally, the prussick knot is tied onto a rope with a closed loop of ¼-inch or 5.5mm. line. The loops range from about 18 inches up to five feet or more, depending on the purpose.

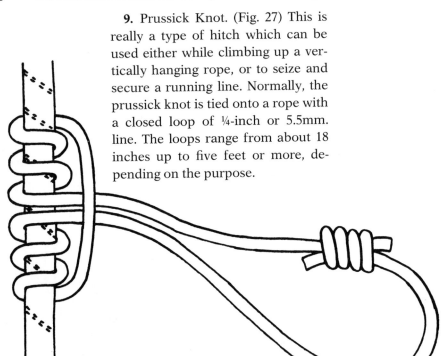

Fig. 27. *Prussick Knot on climbing rope (sling tied with Double Fisherman's Knot).*

Recommended Knots and Applications

(In Webbing)

1. Ring Bend. (Fig. 28) The joining of two ropes or the two ends of one rope is technically known as "bending" them. This knot is similar to the Water Knot, but care must be taken that the webbing is kept flat and smooth as the knot is drawn up.

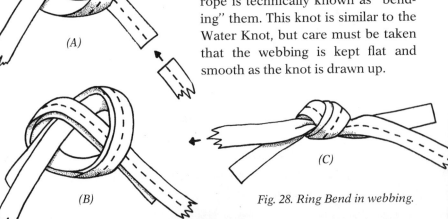

(A)

(B)

(C)

Fig. 28. *Ring Bend in webbing.*

2. Grapevine Knot. (Fig. 29) Adding an extra turn to the Ring Bend produces this knot. It is extra-secure for runners and closed loops made in webbing but can be very difficult to untie once it has "set."

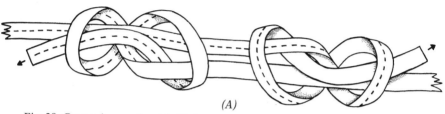

(A)

Fig. 29. Grapevine, or Double Fisherman's, Knot in webbing.

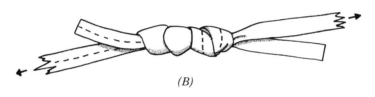

(B)

Other specialized knots are occasionally used for tying up etriers, tightening tent guy lines, or for other purposes.

Besides carabiner on rope, spares hang from web loop.
Prussick loops are tucked into climber's pocket for glacier travel.

chapter 11
Mountain Hardware

CARABINERS

These are steel or aluminum ovals fitted with a spring-loaded gate, used to secure a rope to stationary anchors, yet allowing the line to run through freely. In some situations they are much like pulleys but develop much more friction. Buy them only from reputable climbing shops and use only recognized brands. Only rarely does a carabiner prove to be defective, and even more rarely does one break. However, considering the degree of trust you must place in them, it's wise to purchase the best.

Certain shapes, such as the Chouinard D, are more useful in direct-aid climbing than the standard oval, and are considerably stronger. Steel carabiners are unnecessarily heavy, their extra weight superfluous. An exception might be a rescue situation or a complicated maneuver on steep rock where several heavily loaded lines might be attached to a single anchor. In this case, a heavy steel carabiner with a locking screw collar will contribute to your peace of mind.

HAMMERS

Hammers come in a variety of shapes and weights but one with a reasonably heavy head is best, since fewer swings will be required to drive or remove a piton. Some hammers have a blunt pick, useful for working in hard-to-reach spots, and for placing or retrieving chocks and nuts. Regardless of type, the hammer should be equipped with a cord and shoulder sling to prevent its loss.

HARD HATS

There is no doubt that hard hats are good insurance against concussions and skull fractures. I have seen two

Hard hat can protect climber from falling rock as well as dropped carabiners and other such hardware.

serious accidents that might have been mere incidents had the climbers been wearing protective headgear. Hard hats are not much fun to wear, being disagreeably hot in the summer, heavy and cumbersome in tight spots such as narrow chimneys, and—unless you have different sizes available—difficult to fit over a balaclava during cold weather. However, even where rock is smooth and monolithic, with no loose chunks poised to fall, a dropped carabiner, hammer, nut, or camera can have a profound effect on your climbing style if it strikes you on the head! To be fully protective, a hard hat should have a fairly heavy-gauge outer shell as well as a thick, crushable inner liner, and adequate suspension.

PROTECTION AND ANCHORS

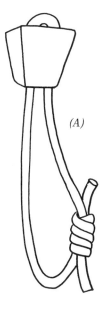

(A)

Chock stones, wedges, nuts, angle irons and "jammables" of all types, as well as slings and runners attached to natural anchors, have virtually replaced pitons as anchoring devices in rock climbing. The repeated use and removal of pitons, especially on popular climbs, has a destructive effect on the relatively fragile rock, and certainly leaves unesthetic scars on the surface patina which may have taken ages to develop. The use of nuts practically eliminates this problem and, in addition, nuts and chocks are more quickly placed where rock is suitable, and normally more easily removed. Certain situations, such as behind

Fig. 30. Here are three types of nuts:
(A) wedge type with 5.5mm nylon cord;
(B) hex type with 9mm rope; and
(C) small wedge type with swaged steel cable.

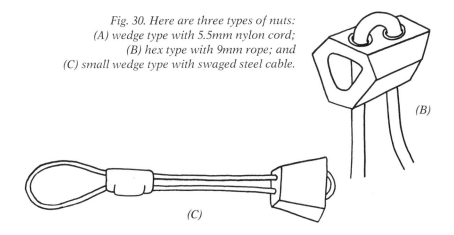

(B)

(C)

an expanding flake, prove that a nut is actually more secure than a well-driven pin. Nuts normally produce no wedging effect on delicately balanced blocks and flakes.

"Clean climbing" with nuts and slings necessitates a more careful approach with regard to the consequences of a fall and the ultimate direction of force on both the nut and the belayer. While this is desirable and can lead to a higher standard of climbing, overzealous use of nuts can lead to problems more severe than the scarring of the rock. It is often difficult to place nuts correctly, particularly where most of the cracks are thin and horizontal. This may prompt inexperienced climbers to forego adequate protection.

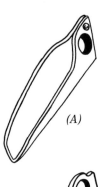

(A)

Also, nuts are often useful in one direction, and unless the climber is very careful not to alter the ultimate direction of force by traversing or placing additional protection in such a way that it torques the nut out of an otherwise secure location, he can easily dislodge one or more of the nuts he has placed behind him.

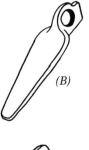

(B)

Pitons, of course, are not foolproof either. They must be placed with care, and a visual inspection is not enough to determine whether or not it is secure. It must be tested! In certain types of rock, such as horizontally thin-bedded quartzites and limestones, flared, smooth-sided vertical cracks, and deep, thin cracks under exfoliated slabs of granite, pitons make the difference between reasonably secure anchors—although causing some damage to the

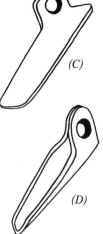

(C)

Fig. 31. Rock pitons are available in a number of styles: (A) medium angle; (B) standard blade (Lost Arrow); (C) bugaboo type; (D) narrow angle; (E) "Realized Ultimate Reality Piton," or RURP; and (F) aluminum bong-bong with large holes to reduce weight.

(D)

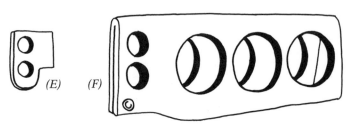

(E)   (F)

rock—and no protection at all. No piece of rock is worth a human life, and each climber must resolve for himself the ethics of clean climbing versus the indiscriminate use of pitons. The ethics and standards of heavily climbed areas should be observed whenever possible, but in questions of this sort, judgment and common sense should prevail.

Only intensive practice in placing and removing nuts and pitons will provide a climber with the judgment necessary to choose the correct size for a crack in question, and to make a reasonably sound assessment of its holding power. Certain fundamentals are to be considered, however, when using either type of protection. Very small nuts and pitons should be used only for direct aid and should not be expected to hold long, hard falls. They simply do not have the surface area needed to resist the shock of heavy loading. Nuts should always be strung with the largest-diameter cord or webbing that will fit in the holes. This should be tied off with a Double Fisherman's Knot in the case of cord, or with a Grapevine Knot when webbing is used. Aircraft cable is used for the smaller sizes but this must be swaged at the factory under strict quality controls.

Angle pitons must always be placed so that their legs are on the same side of the crack and spread toward the final direction of load. Blade-type pitons should be placed so as to avoid excessive torque and leverage and always driven solidly, but without overdriving to the point of warping the eye or weakening its placement by crumbling the rock around it. A piton which bottoms out before it is driven all the way in to the eye will almost certainly fail if subjected to a hard load. A clear, high-pitched ringing sound is normally associated with a well-placed piton but this cannot always be relied upon. The quality of the rock principally determines the holding power of the piton or nut. Therefore, take care that the rock does not crumble to the point of disintegration. Nut runners and slings should be inspected frequently and replaced when they show even slight signs of wear. Nuts which have excessively worn corners can be reshaped with a file, but pitons showing signs of cracking around the eye or along the back of the blade should be discarded.

*Anchoring and belaying are of obvious importance on
routes like Reppy's Crack on Cannon Mountain.*

chapter 12
On the Rocks

BELAYING

"Belay" is a seafaring term meaning to hold and secure. It is the most critical maneuver in climbing—a technique whereby one climber anchors himself and feeds out or takes in rope so that he can safeguard another climber by stopping a fall if that other climber loses his hold.

To understand the importance of belaying, visualize this hypothetical case. You're the second climber on the rope and you've taken a belay stance, with the leader 60 feet above you and a third man 60 feet below you. If the climber below you falls, he may drop only a few inches—

or a few feet if there's slack in the rope. But if the leader falls from 60 feet above you, he can drop that full distance of 60 feet plus another 60, a total of 120 feet, before his rope goes taut below you. Obviously your anchor must be secure, your belay able to withstand a sudden and tremendous strain.

Author is pictured hammering anchor into crack of steep rock slope during direct-aid ascent.

Yet the belaying technique is not especially difficult to learn and, due to the high energy absorption of modern nylon climbing ropes, a fall—though unpleasant—is not as dangerous as it might seem. Still, any fall, whether the drop is a few feet or many, must be considered serious. A falling climber might strike a ledge or other projection, or he might be hit by a rock loosened during the fall. Or something could go wrong with the system of ropes, carabiners, and points of protection. The following precautions should always be observed, whether you're belaying the leader, the second climber on the rope, or any additional climbers.

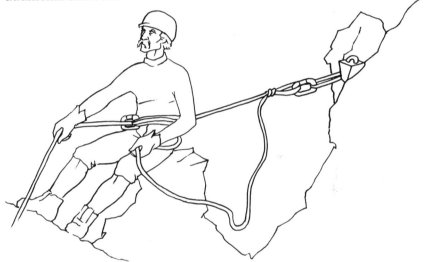

Fig. 32. Drawing shows good belay of second climber.
Note that belayer is tied directly and securely
into anchor with climbing rope by means of butterfly knot.

Regardless of whether positions switch during the course of a climb—and no matter which climber is belaying or being belayed—these precautions are vital:

1. The belayer must always be securely anchored to the mountain so that he cannot be pulled off, no matter what happens! No belay should be attempted until the belayer is satisfied that his anchor will, without question, hold the full weight of two falling men. With experience, and through common sense, you can usually find a suitable anchor. If you can't, don't climb! A large, healthy tree, a solid projecting knob, or several well-placed nuts or pitons may be used. However, where the rock is rotten, the cracks filled with ice and possibly covered by snow, or when working in the dark, setting up a solid anchor may take more than a few minutes. In situations where several nuts or pitons must be placed, the strain of a hard fall can be distributed equally among them by using a system known as a "self-equalizing anchor" (Fig. 33). This can be

Fig. 33. Self-equalizing anchor as pictured here is rigged on two tubular ice screws. Bowline on bight is tied into climbing rope close to belayer, and one of the two loops is enlarged by reducing the other. Small loop is clipped to big one between anchors. This is best way to tie two (or more) anchors together, as it distributes load equally between them, regardless of direction of final pull.

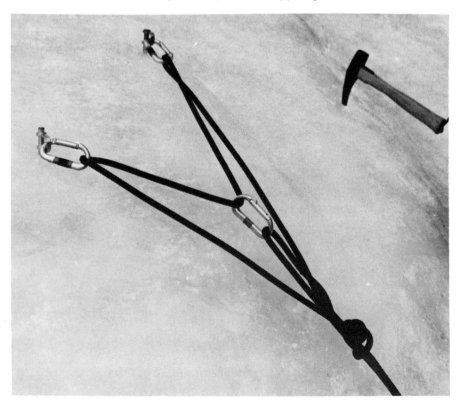

set quickly in most instances by starting with a Bowline on a Bight, tied directly into the climbing line.

2. When belaying, always isolate yourself from the climber and the running line—that is, the rope with which you're belaying him—by tying yourself directly into the anchor with the climbing rope. A situation which **must** be avoided is one where you might be pulled off your belay stance and be stretched out between the anchor and the fallen climber. This can happen more easily than you might think. You can lose control of the belay rope, and all that will save you and the leader will be the rope being brought up sharply and held by either your anchor or your waist. To avoid this, *always* clip your climbing rope to the anchor; *never* tie into that anchor with a separate sling. Tie in with the climbing rope as close to your waist loop or harness as possible while still giving yourself working room.

3. Rig your belay so that you can see the climber for as long as possible. The hand you will use to brake and control a falling climber should be away from the rock, to avoid having your hand wedged between you and the rock, should you be jerked forward suddenly. Control in this position is difficult and you may be forced to let go. Be sure the rope is **under** your tie-in rope if you are belaying the leader; **over** the tie-in rope if you are belaying the second.

4. It's always smart to wear gloves when belaying, or at least a glove on your braking hand. And this is essential when belaying the leader, since he can take the longest fall—from above you to below you. Barehanded, you simply cannot stop a hard fall on a nylon rope.

5. Be certain the rope runs freely as the leader begins to climb by "bird's nesting" it at the belayer's feet where he can reach it easily. This is done by piling it loosely, without any attempt at neat coiling or stacking, beginning with the belayer and working toward the leader. Take every precaution that the rope does not snag under a root or rock beyond the belayer's reach. Should this happen, the leader might be brought up short by a suddenly taut rope, which is disconcerting to say the least if he happens to be in the process of a delicate but imperative move!

Tom Lyman is shown in Durrance Crack, a technical climbing route up vertical wall of Devil's Tower in Wyoming.

6. Clip the running rope to the waist loop or harness on the side opposite from the braking hand with an extra carabiner. This reduces the possibility of the rope being pulled off the belayer's body and out of control if he is flipped upside down, as occasionally happens in trying to brake a hard fall.

7. Above all, pay attention! When you belay, another climber's life is literally in your hands. With experience the belaying technique becomes second nature but don't let this lull you into dangerous inattentiveness. In snubbing a fall, there seems to be no special advantage in allowing the rope to slip slightly through your grip, thus stopping a fall "dynamically." In theory this will soften the shock of a hard fall, but in fact the rope is bound to slip somewhat anyway. Also, the rope's tendency to stretch will soften the fall sufficiently to avoid injury to the climber. The harder the fall, the more the rope will stretch. However, when working on ice, a conscious attempt to allow some slippage in your grip (through your *gloved* hand) might ease the load on questionable anchors and points of protection. Generally, however, hold on firmly and stop the fall as quickly as possible.

8. Signals between the climber and the belayer are important to safety and efficiency. Learn one system and stick with it until the signals become automatic. Keep them as simple as possible; reply immediately, with a minimum of irrelevant conversation which can cause misunderstanding. Also, nothing more quickly destroys the peace and quiet of the mountains or a cliffside than the bellowing that often accompanies a novice climb. Here is a set of signals that work well:

BELAYER: (When he is absolutely sure he is ready to start belaying) "Belay on. Climb away!"
CLIMBER: (Immediately, even if he still has to tie a shoelace, this means that he has heard and understood) "Climbing!"
CLIMBER: (If he wants the belayer to take up more rope, or take it up faster) "Up rope!"

CLIMBER: (If he needs less tension on the line, or extra slack for maneuvering, descending, or traversing) "Slack!"

CLIMBER: (If he needs a taut rope or actual assistance in getting over a difficult spot) "Tension!"

CLIMBER: (To warn a belayer that a "peel" or fall is imminent) "Prepare for Fall!" or "Falling!"

EITHER CLIMBER OR BELAYER: (If rock or any other object has been dislodged, even if you're not certain that it will fall over the edge) "Rock! Rock!"

CLIMBER: (When leading as he clips through various slings or pitons. This gives the belayer some idea of the force to expect in the event of a fall) "Through one! Through two!" etc.

BELAYER: (To confirm that he has heard and understood) "Through one, climb on!" "Through two, climb on!" etc.

Overhangs are among difficult problems of direct-aid climbing on rock walls like this one at Cannon Mountain.

CLIMBER: (After he has reached the belay ledge *and tied in*) "Off belay!"

BELAYER: (Immediately, as a confirmation) "Belay off!"

Rope signals (tugging on the rope) are used occasionally under conditions of high winds or where voices carry poorly. Few climbers need such signals often enough to have memorized any given set, so it is best to improvise your own system on the spot. Signals must be clear, but remember not to tug too hard on the line. More than one climber has been pulled from his stance by an overzealous rope signal.

RAPPELING

Descending steep or overhanging terrain by a controlled slide down a single or double rope is called *"abseiling"* or *"rappeling."* Since the technique is simple and straightforward, it should be relatively safe, yet more climbers are hurt seriously while rappeling than while climbing. This is because rappels are usually made over high-exposure slopes—those which have a greater potential falling distance. Also, while rappeling, you are committed to the rope, not to the rock, and totally dependent on your equipment and a single anchor. The key to rappeling safely lies in making every move slowly and carefully. The following procedure should be carried out when descending "en rappel":

1. Before starting the descent, carefully check the anchor, knots, and your entire rigging. Think about these in terms of what is about to follow. You will swing out away from the face, then drop quickly about 10 feet. Will your rigging, the anchor for example, take the added strain of your sudden stop? A 150-pound climber can easily generate several times that amount of force on a rappel anchor with a sudden stop at the end of a long slide.

2. In tying several ropes together for a descent of 150 feet or more, use only the *Double Sheet Bend*, especially if the ropes are of unequal diameters. Ideally, too, the ropes should be of differing colors for quick identification. Be certain that lines will not jam in a crack as you pull them down after completing a rappel. Also be sure that no loose rock or debris is dislodged by the flailing end of the rope as it passes through or around the anchor.

3. Whether you use one double rope, or two tied together, the free ends should be joined by a Figure-Eight Knot before you throw them down the face. Even if you can see the bottom, get into this habit. It may save your life! Habit could well prevent an oversight.

4. All but the last man down should be fully belayed by a separate rope anchored separately. If you have but two ropes and both are being used for the rappel, tie them off and let the first man go down on a single line, belaying him with the other side. The Figure-Eight Knot will have to be removed in this case and one rope hauled up and "bird's nested" for the belay. The last man down should use a Prussick self-belay, but be sure that it is not too long, in which case it might slip from your hand and jam out of reach. An 18-inch loop is usually sufficient.

This is known appropriately as Direct-Direct Route
for technical climbs up New Hampshire's Cannon Mountain.

5. Go down the ropes smoothly, avoiding the "commando-jump" style of the movies. Such antics strain the anchor and may cause it to fail. You also risk spraining or breaking an ankle as you swing back onto the irregular and unyielding cliff face.

6. While rappeling, have a five-foot Prussick step-in loop readily available. Should something go wrong and you have to stop partway down for any length of time, you can tie the loop into the rappel ropes, then step into it to remove the weight from your shoulder and waist loop. When using a Prussick self-belay, tie the foot loop above the belay loop and remember to take it with you when resuming the descent. Otherwise it will jam the ropes and you won't be able to retrieve them.

7. Double up on all carabiners. If rappeling with a Swiss seat arrangement (Fig. 34) use two carabiners and reverse the gates. This eliminates the possibility of the

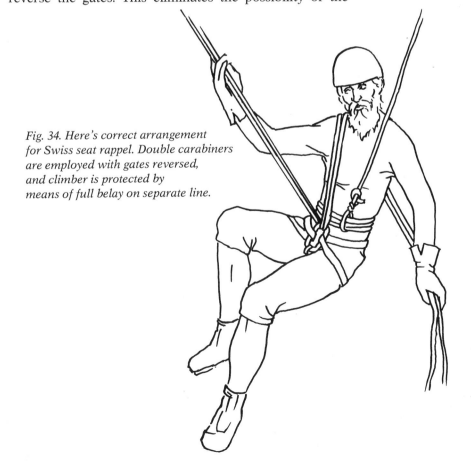

Fig. 34. Here's correct arrangement for Swiss seat rappel. Double carabiners are employed with gates reversed, and climber is protected by means of full belay on separate line.

rope flipping out, since the chance of both gates opening accidentally at the same time is remote. Double up on your anchors as well. If the nuts or pitons are even slightly questionable, use a self-equalizing anchor to distribute the load evenly and don't be afraid to abandon a little equipment to get a sound anchor.

Among the climbing systems, the simplest techniques are usually the safest and most reliable, and this is especially true of rappeling. The simplest method, known as *Dulfersitz*, requires nothing but the rope. To get into the rappel, straddle the doubled rope and grasp this behind you. Bring it around to the front and over the opposite shoulder. Now the rope will be strung under one thigh, around to the front, then diagonally across your chest and over the opposite shoulder. If the rope is over your *left* shoulder, reach behind you with your *right* hand (or vice versa) and grasp the rope with the palm and thumb facing

Fig. 35. Here's Dulfersitz, or body rappel, which requires nothing but climber's rope and is safe, reliable, and simplest rappeling method. Note that separate belay line is tied securely to climber's waist loop.

forward. Now bring the rope forward by your waist and grasp it firmly. This is your controlling and braking hand. Never let go with this hand. The other is used for hanging onto the rope in front, its grasp about neck-high, to provide balance and stability. The feet should be shoulder-width apart and you should bend at the waist so that your torso is nearly vertical with respect to the rock face, and facing directly toward it.

Now lean back until your feet can rest flat, and firmly, against the cliff face. Turn your head only to look over your shoulder to see where you're going. Your legs and guiding hand (the one in front) form a tripod which will keep you stable. A common error is to turn the body too much to one side or the other. Another mistake is to lead down the face with one foot. As you move, this will cause you to swing erratically from side to side. Also, you will not be able to keep feet flat against the face so that you're apt to slip. Make your descent as smooth and continuous as possible. Avoid long leaps, fast drops, and sudden stops. These transmit excessive stress to anchor points.

At the top, as you start your rappel, cry out loudly: "On rappel!" Shout it so that the belayer, and anyone at the bottom, understands you. Signal that you are completely clear of both the rappel and belay lines by yelling: "Off rappel!" when you reach the bottom. Following these basic procedures will simplify the operation and contribute to everyone's safety.

A second type of rappel, commonly used, requires an 8½-foot sling of one-inch webbing, tied off with a Water or Grapevine Knot. The length of the webbing may vary, but for most climbers, eight to nine feet will produce a closed loop that fits comfortably around the pelvis. Place the knot at the small of the back and bring both ends of the loop around to the front from either side. Then reach through the legs, and bring the third loop through the crotch, diaper-like. This forms a basket or harness around the hips and pelvic structure forming, in effect, a seat.

All three loops are held with one hand and clipped together with *two* carabiners, side by side with the gates opening in the same direction. Now, clip the doubled rappel rope through these carabiners so that it forms a right-angle bend as it goes over the shoulder. Then reverse one of the carabiners so that both gates cannot be opened simultaneously by accident. The rappel is accomplished in the same manner as with the rope directly through the crotch and under the thigh, except that the sling, known as a *Swiss seat* or *diaper seat*, eliminates rope friction on the leg, transferring this to the carabiners. The descent will be more comfortable but somewhat faster, since friction is reduced. This is, however, a better technique when the rappel is made from an overhang and your full weight is carried by the rope.

A third variation involves placing a brake bar on the waist loop or in conjunction with the Swiss seat. This takes all of the weight off the climber's body and is consequently more comfortable. Be advised, however, that brake bars are hard on rope, and care must be taken not to descend too rapidly, as friction will heat the carabiners to the extent of damaging the rope, or possibly burning yourself! This system is good for long descents on fixed lines, or when ropes are apt to be wet or icy. Gloves must be worn and the rope must be brought back around the small of the back to the front and controlled by the opposite hand to provide additional friction and braking.

CLIMBING AND MOVING ON ROCK

Much has been written and spoken concerning the physical and mental exercises involved in rock climbing. Various experts and authorities have described and demonstrated, repeatedly, how to cling to insignificant rugosities and miniscule flakes, muscle over ceilings and overhanging slabs, and ascend "impossible" off-width cracks. However, what works for these experts may not work for you. On the other hand, there is no reason why you cannot successfully develop an entirely new approach to any given problem on a boulder or face. In rock climbing, there are a few fundamental rules, applicable to everyone, novice and expert alike. Beyond these, skill must be developed in relation to your own native ability, physique and strength, and above all, your mental commitment and desire to climb. Mental discipline and control become increasingly

*Author climbs Southwest Ridge of Storm Point
in Grand Teton National Park, Wyoming.*

important as climbing becomes more of an art and less of an exercise in technical ability.

Perhaps the two most important factors of safe and successful climbing on ice, snow, or rock are balance and conservation of energy. Basically, climbing is modified walking. The vertical and irregular nature of a rock face demands certain adjustments in stride and speed but, nonetheless, rock climbing should be done mainly with the feet and legs. Only the most demanding moves require more than an occasional assist from the hands, arms, and back. The body is lifted upward by the large muscles of the legs; it is not pulled up with the relatively small arm muscles. A good sense of balance is necessary to keep this upward thrust by the legs effectively centered under the body's center of gravity. To illustrate, try standing a few inches from a chair, placing one foot on the seat. Keeping the body vertical, try to lift yourself up by pushing with that foot. It can't be done. Yet if you stand very close to the chair and lean over it slightly, you can easily lift your-self straight up with the thrust of one leg. Almost every move in climbing can be defined in terms of similar bal-ance and expenditure of energy.

Rock climbing can be divided roughly into two types: face climbing, and interior or counterforce climbing. Face climbing is almost totally an exercise in balance and men-tal adjustment to exposure. Each step up, down, or across should be smooth and not overly long. Occasionally, you will be forced to make a wide, spread-eagle traverse to reach an only existing hold, but these strides are tiring and tend to throw you off balance. On very steep faces the hands grasp whatever holds are available for safety in case the foot slips. This three-point suspension should be maintained wherever possible. You should climb with your eyes, too, keeping them several moves ahead to avoid ending up in a cul-de-sac, or finding yourself sud-denly on rotten rock. Where the hands are used for safety and balance, they should be rested lightly against the rock to avoid burning up excessive energy by gripping each hold so tightly that the knuckles turn white. When the arms are needed to assist the legs over an awkward spot, the move should be smooth and quick, again to conserve energy. *Never* jump or lunge for a hold. If it breaks, or if you miss, your chances of a fall are good!

Keep the body away from the rock, consistent with comfort, but not to the extent that your butt becomes the most prominent overhang on the rock. Stand far enough away so that you can locate footholds and yet be able to move smoothly and efficiently. Also, unless the rock is ac-tually vertical or overhangs, keeping your body away from the rock will insure that your center of gravity is directly over your feet.

Friction is what holds your feet to the rock. The greater the weight on them, the better your boot soles will grip. All rock climbing involves this friction but the technique of climbing smooth, low-to-moderate-angle slabs involves several refinements in the use of the feet. This is referred to as *friction climbing*. Balance is everything. You must keep your full weight over your feet. Unless the slab is very steep and you touch the rock with one hand for balance and support, your feet are your only contact with the mountain. If you give way to the tendency to lean toward the rock, your center of gravity will shift and your feet will slide out from under you. Because friction is so important, try to bend your ankles so that the soles of your shoes are flat against the rock at all times. This can be done by keeping your feet pointed (either up- or downhill) at an angle of about 45 degrees. Never place your foot horizontally across a slope since it will tend to roll, with a consequent loss of friction. In a variation of this technique, one foot is kept flat at 45 degrees while the other toes straight into the rock, keeping as much of the front sole on the rock as possible.

Downclimbing on friction also requires maximum contact with the rock (not, however, on the seat of your pants). Remain upright and center your weight over your feet. You can fall a long way on friction slabs without injury, but only if you make a sliding fall. Never allow yourself to tumble or roll. Always be ready to slide on your back. On wet or mossy rock there is little you can do to help yourself, but on dry rock try to shift your weight, at least partially, to your feet and allow your shoes to take most of the wear and abrasion. Keep your face and palms away from the rock surface.

Inside corners, jamcracks, and chimneys are normally climbed with a technique involving methods used in both types of climbing, face and interior. Occasionally, where rock is exceptionally smooth, pure counterforce must be applied to climb and to hold yourself on the rock. Counterforce calls for pushing or pulling in different directions with arms and legs, and the jamming of elbows, knees, legs, and fists into appropriate cracks. Both these techniques are simply ways of holding yourself on the rock. In order to move upward, one limb at a time is raised, with which you either pull, push, or jam yourself into a higher position. Balance is still vital, but because muscles are continually working either actively or statically, this type of climbing can be very exhausting. Great strength is normally required but even here a climber learns to apply only enough force to keep himself in position, conserving as much energy as possible. Jamming is an effective technique but a climber should use caution, since a sudden slip can lodge a knee, fist, or leg painfully into a flaring crack.

The *layback* is perhaps the most strenuous move of all and involves pushing with the feet and pulling with the hands on opposite sides of offset cracks. On very steep or overhanging cracks, few climbers can keep this up for long.

The *retable* or *mantleshelf* involves reaching up with the arms, and with a combination of pull from the arms and spring from the feet, lifting yourself over a ceiling or overhang. As the chest comes up to the level of the hands, the upper body is rolled forward. Then the arms are straightened, lifting the body high enough so that one foot can be placed on the shelf next to the hands. If the mantleshelf is accomplished smoothly and quickly, it does not require an inordinate amount of strength. However, if the shelf is too narrow to permit the chest to be hunched in over the hands, most of the work must be done by the arms, the body being held in position until one leg can be swung high enough to take some of the weight.

Try to place the *foot* flatly on the ledge, *not* the knee. At times you may have no choice, but because the knee is round it is apt to slip, throwing you off balance and to one side. Also, the knee is easily bruised. In addition, you cannot move to a higher position while on your knees. You need at least one foot under you for sufficient leverage to stand. With practice you will find that you can place one foot into almost any position where you might be tempted to place your knee.

Many climbing problems require a simultaneous combination of several techniques and only with extensive practice can you judge the force necessary to keep yourself wedged in a steep jamcrack, or at exactly what point on a steep friction slab gravity will overcome the adhesion of your bootsoles. Varying conditions of temperature and humidity greatly affect the ability of rubber soles to "stick" to rock. Beware of water on the surface, lichens and mosses, pine needles, and glacially polished sections. These can be exceedingly slippery.

ROUTEFINDING ON ROCK

Skill in routefinding comes only with practice on all types of rock under various conditions. A route that appears perfectly feasible in clear, dry weather may prove difficult, even treacherous, under cold, wet, or windy conditions. A series of tempting cracks, ledges, or other irregularities which an optimist might consider negotiable is referred to as a *line*. The straighter and more direct the proposed route is, the more difficult it generally is; also the greater its appeal! A route that proceeds directly from the bottom of a face to the top, with a minimum of traversing and wandering about, is known as a *directissima*.

Generally, an ascent route is determined by the leader since he must be the first to cope with individual problems. An area or line is usually decided upon by observing the overall condition of the cliff and the type of rock involved, determining the number and availability of ledges which might be suitable for belays and bivouacs, and by making a rough estimate of the length of the climb, and the time which will be required. A half-hour or more on your back with a pair of binoculars will provide a careful study of the face, revealing hidden details and saving considerable "fumbling around" during the actual climb. Only very general advice can be given for routefinding as each cliff, wall, or mountain has its own special features and peculiarities, and of course, experienced climbers purposely seek the unusual and challenging!

Climbers of moderate experience, however, should keep the following points in mind, whether considering a previously climbed and well-known route or an intriguing but unknown line:

1. Undoubtedly the greatest danger in rock climbing is loose or rotten rock. Keep away from it. Often the merest touch of a critically wedged piece will dislodge a number of adjacent pieces. Also, it is difficult to establish reliable belay anchors and points of protection on such surfaces. Whenever rotten rock *must* be climbed, or when it is encountered unexpectedly, use every possible precaution to avoid dislodging even the smallest piece. Falling rock has a way of ricocheting at unexpected angles, possibly striking your rope or the belayer. When you encounter rotten or loose rock, avoid it by traversing or back off from it while you still can.

Skillful routefinding is needed on such challenging faces as Symmetry Spire in Tetons, but beware of rotten rock.

2. Avoid climbing directly over large overhangs. Falling from such a projection makes it difficult to get back to the rock face. You'll dangle in space. If your route does force an overhang traverse, be certain to have a Prussick step-in loop readily available. This is a five-foot loop, tied in a ¼-inch (5.5mm.) line which can be attached to the climbing rope at about head height. By threading this through your waist loop and stepping into it with one or both feet, you can completely remove your weight from the waist loop and hang comfortably in space for as long as necessary. Without this Prussick step-in loop, your waist loop will slowly work its way up around your diaphragm and rib cage, causing suffocation within 15 to 20 minutes.

Occasionally, bad weather or other difficulty will force you to retreat. Should a direct descent be blocked by a big overhang, valuable time can be lost trying to traverse around one side of it before a rappel or downclimb can be continued.

3. Anticipate the type of climbing you will encounter by becoming familiar with various kinds of rock before actually undertaking the climb. Exfoliating granite slabs may provide a greater variety of holds than will be found in horizontally bedded quartzites or vertically jointed limestones. Viewing the cliff from different angles and under varying light conditions may also reveal a great deal more information than does a head-on view at high noon.

4. Locate alternate lines adjacent to your proposed route and possible avenues of escape should this become necessary. Occasionally, prominent ledge systems traversing the entire width of the face may provide an easy out in the event of accident or bad weather. More likely, however, retreat will probably have to be accomplished by a combination of rappels and downclimbing. An experienced climber never leaves himself without an escape route.

5. Remember that rappels need not always be vertical descents. Often it is possible for the first man to *pendulum,* or swing well to one side, to find a suitable anchor for the next rappel. I can recall several occasions when it was necessary to descend at angles as much as 45 degrees in order to reach alcoves or ledges on which to set up the next rappel.

In short, good routefinding includes contingency plans for possible forced descents or the evacuation of an injured climber. Should you be caught on a cliff after dark, it is usually advisable to wait until daylight before finishing the last pitch or continuing the descent. The possibility of accidents increases markedly at night. Still, if caught without adequate clothing, or if someone needs immediate medical attention, you may have no alternative to a nighttime descent. In that case, a clear mental image of the cliff's features and your position on it may be the only factors working in your favor!

ESTABLISHING PROTECTION WHILE LEADING

Leading on rock or ice is vastly more dangerous and requires much greater experience than following as a second or third climber. In the event of a fall, the leader will almost certainly drop several feet, possibly a considerable distance, even if the rope system works perfectly and the belayer handles his job with precision. The second or third climber, on the other hand, is belayed from above and is accorded almost perfect protection since he can fall but a few inches at most if the leader is attentive and belays him properly. It is important, then, that as the leader climbs, he clip his rope into solid anchors and points of protection every 10 to 15 feet, depending upon the difficulty of the climb. In so doing, he limits his potential fall to double the length of the rope above his last, and usually highest, point of protection.

These points are normally pitons, carefully placed nuts, wedges, and "jammables" of various types, or nylon slings or *runners* looped around solid flakes or knobs, natural chockstones, or healthy trees. The correct placement of these has already been discussed.

With regard to points of protection, there is little mystery about the proper placing of these, or the use of natural anchors, but it should be reemphasized that they must

be absolutely solid. Climbers may sometimes find it difficult to establish solid anchors, so they are tempted to insert what they refer to as "psychological" nuts or pitons,
knowing full well that these may not hold but feeling that
such anchors impart mental reassurance required to
handle the next demanding move. These marginal or inadequate anchors serve only to give a climber a false
sense of security and increase the chances of a system
foul-up should a fall occur.

One poor anchor close to another still adds up only to
two poor anchors, and if subjected to heavy loading by a
long fall will simply fail in succession. Occasionally it is
possible to distribute the load exactly in half on two marginal points of protection with a self-equalizing rigging.
However, simply looping a continuous sling through two
or more piton eyes or nut slings will in no way increase
their security. Under stress, the weakest point will fail
first, followed by the others in quick succession.

*This exercise in direct-aid climbing on Devil's Tower
in Wyoming is known as the Hollywood and Vine Route.*

Protection for the leader during a fall derives from the energy-absorbing qualities of the rope and from the belayer's ability to stop the fall—not from multitudinous points of protection. Too many nuts or pitons, especially on a complicated pitch that calls for much traversing and zigzagging, can bind the rope too closely to the rock, resulting in so much drag that the leader will find it difficult to move, and the belayer will experience an inadequate feel for the leader's movements. Some friction over smooth rock and through carabiners is desirable, of course, since this, too, helps absorb energy produced by a fall. It also reduces the strain on the belayer. But too much friction can offset much of the rope's ability to absorb shock. Then, too, excessive friction increases the chance of a malfunction in the system.

On all but the first lead or pitch, where the climbers actually start from the ground level, the leader should place some solid protection immediately, before he moves some distance from the belayer. If he should fall on a steep sec-

Author's wife makes her way carefully up exfoliating granite slabs of Whitehorse Ledge in New Hampshire.

tion after having climbed 20 feet or more without protection, the full weight of his fall will bear directly on the belayer. Avoid this by insisting that the leader immediately clip into something solid, at the beginning of each pitch.

Friction in a rope system can be reduced without decreasing the security of its attachments to the rock by the use of *runners*. These are usually slings of one-inch nylon webbing tied off with a Water or Grapevine Knot. Short slings, 18 to 20 inches in length, are looped into nut slings or clipped to piton eyes with carabiners and serve to reduce the acute angles which can form in the climbing rope where points of protection must be awkwardly located under overhangs or within deep, inside corners. Most experienced climbers use runners consistently to reduce rope drag behind them, and to keep the rope from running tightly over sharp corners. Longer webbing slings, sometimes up to 10 feet or more in length, can be looped over solid blocks, around trees, or around natural chockstones to provide solid protection while still allowing the rope certain flexibility and reducing friction.

There is no rule of thumb when it comes to the number or spacing of points of protection. A leader should simply use as many, or as few, as he feels are necessary. On steep rock of moderate difficulty, protection points should probably be established at least every 15 feet or so, thus limiting a potential fall to 30 feet. Most climbers agree that a fall of this magnitude is sufficiently thrilling! On smooth slabs or easy rock, much greater distances can safely be left between points of protection. Occasionally, an entire pitch or lead of 150 feet can be climbed with nothing more than a solid belay anchor and perhaps a single intermediate anchor.

A leader, however, must be constantly aware of the nature of the rock below him onto which he could fall. Often, protection is required, not so much to hold him to the mountain, but rather to redirect the belay and keep him from striking a particularly sharp or rotten section. It is important, too, to keep in mind that the second climber may require protection as he begins or ends a long traverse. This is especially true in a situation where a falling

*Exfoliating granite looks difficult but may have more
holds than jointed limestone or horizontally bedded quartzite.*

second climber could pendulum out over a large overhang. Even if not injured, it might prove most difficult for
him to return to the face of the rock.

Beyond the necessity for establishing physical protection and finding a suitable route, the leader must always be conscious of the strength and resolve of the rest
of the rope team. Serious trouble could develop if the second or third climber becomes exhausted just below the
crux move which the leader may surmount only with difficulty. There is also a natural tendency among members

of a team to suspend their own judgment and intuition, relying instead entirely on the leader to make all decisions regarding time, weather, strength of the party, and the choice of a route. Each member must be willing to contribute advice, ideas, and opinions based on his own judgment and experience, while still working toward a common goal, and acknowledging the role of the leader.

Finally, remember that climbing is a hollow accomplishment if it is not enjoyed. It can, and frequently does, involve discomfort, wet, cold, and moments of anxious deliberation, but when it becomes obviously dangerous and genuine fear replaces anxiety, it is time to retreat. Learn to recognize your physical and mental limits. Push them from below occasionally, to be sure, but don't extend yourself so far that climbing loses all meaning and sense of proportion. The point in climbing is **not** to fall or to get hurt. Remember, there's always another day, and another mountain waiting.

Extremely large, deep crevasse on Mount Logan in Yukon has overhanging lips that are deceptive and dangerous.

chapter 13
Snow and
Ice Climbing

Although many of the techniques, and much of the equipment used on rock, are similar to or adaptable to those
utilized in ice and snow climbing, the very nature of the
latter calls for a wholly different approach and attitude on
the part of the climber. Routes and climbs on rock vary
little from year to year, and certainly their characteristics
and peculiarities don't change from day to day, or from
minute to minute. But this is not true of ice and snow.
When climbing on these, remember that you are climbing
on water, its apparent solidity totally dependent upon an
air temperature below freezing. Considered in this light,

snow and ice are mobile, plastic media, the very antithesis of a granite batholith or a 200-million-year-old limestone reef.

Climbing difficulties on snow and ice are compounded by the generally colder, windier, and more demanding conditions of winter weather and higher elevations. The necessity for warmer and more cumbersome clothing, in addition to the colder temperatures, requires a greater expenditure of energy merely to exist and function. It is usually impossible to place anchors in snow and ice which provide the near-perfect security of anchors set in rock. A fall on steep snow or ice can be as serious as a similar one on rock. Evacuation of an injured climber is hampered by cold and wind, and it often becomes a race against time. Finally, blocks of snow and chunks of ice have a way of detaching themselves from the mountain at unexpected and inappropriate moments. Ice avalanches and snow slides are an ever-present hazard, and evidence of the relative instability of water in its frozen state. All in all, climbing under winter conditions is much more of an art than a science; real skill and judgment are gained only through many active climbing seasons—that is, through experience.

CLIMBING ON SNOW

Two great dangers associated with climbing on snow and ice are avalanches and *hypothermia*. The metabolic condition known as hypothermia (literally a subnormal body temperature) can result in injury or even death. It's a severe form of exposure. Because the dangers both of avalanches and hypothermia are so real, so important, these topics will be treated separately in the chapter on climbing hazards. For the moment simply bear in mind that safety precautions are of prime concern when dealing with snow and ice.

Due to the increased weight of winter clothing and equipment, it is vital to maintain an even pace and to conserve energy. More so than in rock climbing, moving on snow and ice is basically a form of walking, adjusted to steeper angles. On soft snow, steps can usually be kicked

straight into the snow, or stamped into horizontal plat-
forms along the slope. On hard-packed snow or on ice, the
technique of climbing becomes similar to that employed
on smooth-friction slabs. Again, balance is important, and
ankles must be bent enough to allow at least one foot to
rest flatly against the surface. A technique that is straightforward and conserves energy is to place one foot flat
against the slope, pointing uphill at about 45 degrees,
while the other foot is toed straight into the slope. The position of the feet can be alternated, of course, equalizing
the strain on leg muscles. It is much easier to maintain a
slow and steady pace on snow than on rock but, even
more important, energy must be conserved and stumbling
avoided.

Leaning on ice axe, author leads party up steep,
slippery ice of New Hampshire's Frankenstein Cliff.

Wherever possible, steep snow slopes and couloirs should be climbed straight up or at a very steep angle to avoid producing a line of weakness across the slope. A horizontal line of footprints traversing a steep slope can lead to a fracturing of the snow layers and the formation of a slab avalanche. If such a slope must be crossed, it should be done quickly, as a series of short horizontal traverses, connected by vertical sections at right angles to the general direction of travel. Crossing in this manner greatly reduces the chance of starting a massive slab avalanche.

Always climb away from the fall line of prominent blocks and cornices, since these frequently fall for no apparent reason. Attempting to tunnel through a snow cornice is risky at best. The line of fracture behind a cornice is invariably at least half again farther back than the actual overhang (Fig. 36). The sides of a couloir, or U-shaped slope, are obviously safer than the center should you be caught in a small snowslide. Solid overhangs offer the

Fig. 36. Cornice of snow and rime ice is formed over sharp rock ridge by strong prevailing winds; dotted line indicates possible line of fracture. Always stay well back from edge of suspected cornice overhangs.

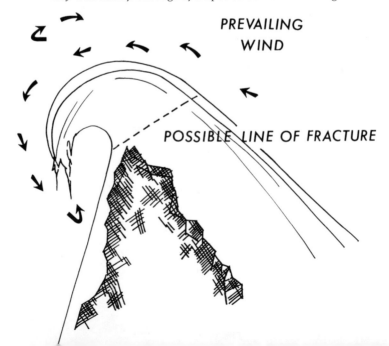

PREVAILING WIND

POSSIBLE LINE OF FRACTURE

only real protection against large avalanches in gullies or on open faces.

TOOLS FOR SNOW AND ICE CLIMBING

Whereas rock climbing may require little more than a rope for safety, snow or ice climbing necessitates specialized tools for protection and to provide a climber with purchase on a hard and usually slippery surface.

The Ice Axe: The primary tool is the ice axe. It's a cutting tool consisting of an adze and a pick, *both of which should be kept sharp.* Any cutting instrument is safer and more efficient if kept sharp. Ice can be cut easily with a sharp axe, but trying to gouge or shatter it with a blunt instrument is a waste of time and energy. Those who question the wisdom of a sharp axe and crampons feel, that in a fall, sharp edges can be dangerous as they flail about uncontrollably. However, a fall in itself is a supreme hazard, one that can often be prevented by use of a sharp ice axe.

The head of the axe should comprise a straight, flat adze with square corners. The pick should be long, at least seven inches, and slightly curved to allow the force of a blow to fall on the point of the pick as the axe follows the arc of swing. A carabiner hole is sometimes provided on an axe and sometimes this is useful, but never in belaying. The spike at the other end of the shaft should be two and a half to three inches long and *must* have a square or rectangular—not round—cross section. A round spike will pull free when side pressure is applied to the shaft. The smoother the juncture at the metal ferrule which joins the handle and spike, the more easily the axe shaft can be thrust into hard-packed snow.

The shaft itself may be either of wood or metal. Wood (and various laminates) are lighter, more resilient, and dampen the vibrations or shock created by chopping. In addition, wood and composition shafts are more esthetically pleasing, and while this is not as important as strength and serviceability, it is an important consideration for many climbers. Metal, on the other hand, offers superior strength. With modern plastic and rubber coatings, an ice-cold handle is not a serious problem, nor is the tendency for metal to ice up. Excessive weight is the main disadvantage of a metal shaft. Probably only titanium would provide a strength-to-weight ratio similar to that of laminated wood but the price would be astronomical. Ash is the least serviceable and most commonly found wood on cheaper axes. Hickory is little better, and heavier yet. Shafts of laminated wood or bamboo seem to offer the best compromise among weight, strength, and esthetic appeal. Whatever type of shaft you decide upon, the weakest point is where the tines of the axe head are riveted to the shaft. There should be three rivets, and the head must meet the shaft at a true 90-degree angle. Check shaft and fittings for overall workmanship. Also, test the shaft for strength. It should, when propped between two objects, support your full weight. If a salesman refuses to permit such a test, don't buy his axe!

An ice axe should be provided with a means for attaching it to yourself, with a line or thong. If you lose your axe irretrievably—in a deep crevasse, for example—you minimize your very chances for survival since you'll have no tool with which to belay or make a self-arrest! The wrist strap and glide rings supplied with most new axes should be replaced if you feel you can improve on them. Short axes for difficult climbs are usually rigged by climbers with special wrist loops which are used more for support than for loss prevention. Length can be determined by choosing an axe that reaches from your *wrist*—not your palm!—to the floor as you stand normally. Traditionally it has been recommended that it reach from your palm to the floor, but I find this too short. Ice-axe lengths are usually denoted in centimeters, 85 cm. being about right for a person 5 feet 10 inches tall. A 70-cm. axe is standard for ice climbing, shorter ones occasionally being used for steep climbs in very narrow gullies.

At least once each season a wood shaft should be lightly sanded and rubbed with boiled linseed oil as a rot preventive, and for the sake of appearance. Cutting edges can be touched up with a flat, mill-bastard file. Don't use a grinding wheel. This will draw the temper from the steel, softening the edge and causing discoloration.

Crampons: Crampons are assemblies of sharp spikes mounted on lightweight metal frames which, when strapped securely to climbing boots, provide purchase and traction on hard snow or on ice. They are available with either 10- or 12-point projections on each frame. The 12-point type is essential for serious mountaineering and ice climbing. In both cases, 10 points are oriented vertically from the foot (directly downward) but when crampons are equipped with two additional points, these project *forward horizontally* from the toe. The vertical points grip when the sole of the boot is placed flat on the ice or snow surface, while the two horizontal "horns" are intended to be driven directly into steep ice. There are hybrids—10-point crampons having two forward points angled toward the front at 45 degrees—but these are generally less effective than either the 10- or 12-point models. A four-point instep crampon, commonly sold as an "ice gripper," is totally unsatisfactory for mountain work.

Fig. 37. These 12-point crampons are Chouinard rigid adjustable type (top) and hinged semi-adjustable Salewa.

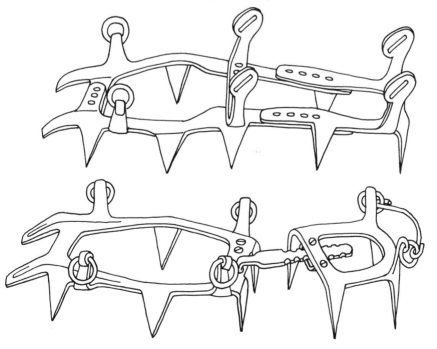

The crampon frame is equipped with six or more short upright posts, or grips, each having a slot or flexible ring to accommodate a strap which, in turn, holds the crampon to the boot. These rings should be designed so that they do not flop over and catch under the boot as the crampons are being attached. Slots in the rear posts serve as well as rings, but the front posts must have rings to facilitate threading straps through them while you're wearing gloves. On adjustable crampons there is sometimes a heel wire connecting the two rear posts. This wire limits foot slippage along the frame. Once the crampon is properly fitted to your boot, have the wire spot-welded or brazed in proper position. This will later save much fumbling with cold or mittened hands. It guarantees a permanent, and correct, fit without further adjustment.

Crampon frames are either flexibly hinged or fully rigid. The rigid type is superior for difficult technical ice climbing where frequent use is made of the front projecting horns. Such a frame tends to stiffen the boot and provide a more solid platform on which to stand. "Front pointing" up a steep slope on the front horns can be extremely tiring, and the extra rigidity of this frame reduces muscle fatigue. But in order to make the most effective use of the solid frame, it should be worn only on very stiff boots. Technical ice-climbing boots normally have thick, rigid midsoles that defy flexing, at least during the first season or two.

The hinged crampon is superior in all other situations. Because it bends with the foot, walking over smooth terrain is more comfortable. Hinged 12-point crampons are satisfactory for occasional short pitches on the steepest ice.

Most modern crampons are at least partially adjustable, not so much to adapt to several different boots, but to enable you to get a perfect fit, which is essential. Once you have made the necessary adjustments, the crampon should cling to the boot, held there by pressure of the grips on the sole, even without straps.

Years of experimenting with various means for attaching crampons to boots have failed to produce a truly efficient and convenient harness. The best to date is the two-strap system. I do not recommend the use of a single, long strap, especially one which is wrapped around the leg above the ankle. This arrangement restricts blood circulation to the feet. Tightening the strap is difficult, too. Neoprene is superior to nylon or cloth for straps, while nickel-plated, heavy-duty buckles hold more firmly than the various sliding-type fasteners which are supposed to grip anywhere along the strap. Use a leather punch to make the holes for the buckle tongue, adding a few extra ones in each direction to accommodate stretch in the strap, or so you can easily shift holes when you encounter difficulty due to icy fittings or cold hands.

Rappeling on ice is no problem with proper equipment, as shown here on Mount Monadnock in New Hampshire.

Along with the ice axe, crampons are essential for travel above timberline, or on any winter slope. Crampons, too, are cutting tools, and the points should be kept needle-sharp. Like a dull axe or knife, blunt-pointed crampons are dangerous. They cannot be relied on to grip efficiently. So that the sharp points won't puncture or damage other equipment when they're carried in your pack, cover the points with rubber "spider" protectors. Be sure, too, to carry extra allen keys and wrenches with your adjustable crampons, along with extra screws and nuts.

Anchors for Snow: Ice axes are usually the only implement with which a belay anchor can be established in snow, although expeditionary climbers carry **pickets** used to set up permanent anchors for fixed lines. These are three- to four-foot aluminum tubes, or T-angle shafts, sometimes equipped with a carabiner hole, or a short wire or nylon loop. In soft snow these can be buried lengthwise to serve as a "deadman" anchor. However, in hard-packed snow, they are driven vertically, like pitons. Pickets are often used in pairs, one backing up the other. With these, the self-equalizing anchor can be used to bear the load equally where this seems advisable.

Recently, the use of *flukes* has become more popular. These are triangular metal pads, with a wire cable sling or a nylon loop attached slightly off-center. Buried in the snow at the proper angle, these tend to dig deeper and deeper as downhill force is applied to them. Only when the resistance against the compacted snow is equal to the force of a fall do they stop "digging." Some experience is needed to position them effectively.

In soft snow, several pickets, ice axes, skis, even ski poles and snowshoes, can be buried to form "deadmen." Once the snow is packed firmly about them, these will resist considerable loading.

Anchors in Ice: Tubular ice pitons, barbed pitons, or ice screws are normally necessary to establish secure anchors in ice. Pitons and screws are started with a hammer and must be placed carefully to avoid shattering or cracking the ice. Ice pitons should be hammered rapidly with light

taps to "melt" them into the ice rather than being driven
with heavy blows as one drives a nail into a plank. Each
blow of the hammer should drive the piton a mere eighth-
inch at a time. This allows the point to melt the ice under
pressure and lessens the chances of splitting off a large
flake. Ice screws are started with a hammer, too, then
turned slowly by hand for the same reason.

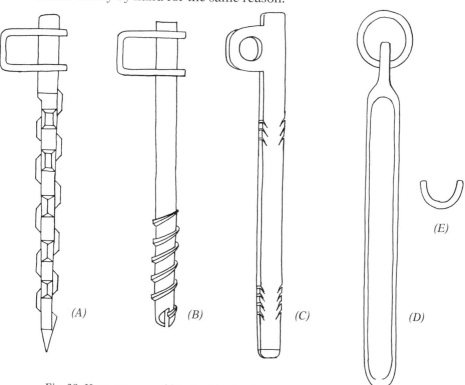

Fig. 38. Here are several kinds of ice hardware:
(A) wart-hog type of ice piton; (B) tubular ice screw;
(C) Austrian (barbed-shank) ice piton; and
(D) half-tube piton for soft ice. For calarity, shank
of half-tube is also shown in cross-section (E).

When spotting ice pitons or screws, the surface should
first be cleared of snow, then broken up with the axe. This
softens the surface, making it easier to start the piton or
the screw. In extremely hard water-ice which has formed
in layers, this approach will also relieve some of the stress
on the upper layers, and lessen their tendency to crack
and split.

Both types of anchors—pitons or ice screws—should be placed at a 10-degree uphill angle (Fig. 39). On steep ice, small steps or pockets must be cut, in which to place the anchors. Otherwise they will be too close to the surface.

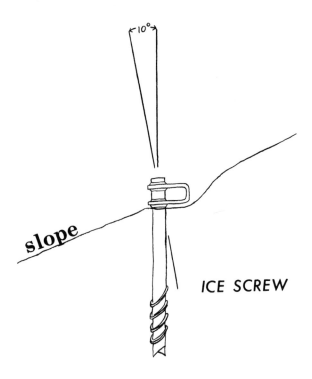

Fig. 39. Where possible, ice screw or piton is driven not quite perpendicular to slope but at very slight uphill angle. Loop forming eye is on uphill side; carabiner will be clipped directly to barrel or shaft.

The strength of ice hardware depends on placing it so that there is approximately an 80-degree angle between the axis of the anchor and the direction of loading. There is little, if any, holding power when the load is closely in line with, or parallel to, the axis. Where ice anchors must remain in place for several hours they should be covered with compacted snow or ice chips to insulate them against infrared rays from sun which, when absorbed into the metal, melt the snow, and therefore, loosen. This can happen even on a cloudy day.

On steep slopes, double up on the anchors, placing them at least two feet apart with one slightly uphill of the other. Again, use a *self-equalizing anchor* to distribute the load.

Ice screws and pitons should have a fairly wide cross section to provide sufficient lateral resistance against ice. Avoid using anchors which appear to be made of steel wire, and those whose shafts are less than ⅜-inch thick.

Eyes are welded to some ice screws and pitons, while metal rings or loops are rigged on others so that they pivot about the shaft. The latter are usually inadequate to stop a hard fall. A better system consists of a carabiner or sling, clipped or looped directly to the shaft of the piton with the eye pointing uphill and acting as a keeper to prevent the carabiner or sling from coming off (Fig. 40).

Lacking ice pitons or screws, ice mushrooms or *bollards* can be cut into homogeneous ice as rappel anchors, but

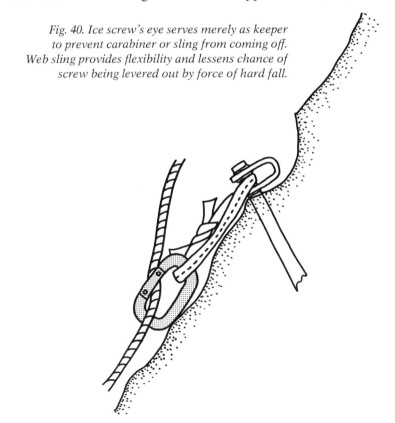

Fig. 40. Ice screw's eye serves merely as keeper to prevent carabiner or sling from coming off. Web sling provides flexibility and lessens chance of screw being levered out by force of hard fall.

these must be used with extreme care. The notch behind the mushroom must be slanted inward at 10 degrees, and be deep enough to insure that the rope cannot slip off accidentally (Fig. 41).

Fig. 41. As improvised rappel anchor, notch is cut into ice and rope is looped around resulting bollard, or "mushroom." Slot is angled and deep to prevent slipping.

The Ice Hammer: An ice hammer is necessary on all serious ice routes, and proves useful in snow climbing as well. For example, a hammer is often needed for driving pickets into hard-packed snow. On steep pitches or in ice gullies, the only way to establish secure anchors for belaying may require several well-placed pitons driven into rock walls along the sides of a gully. Where *verglas,* a coating of ice over rock, is encountered, a hammer is more useful than an axe for locating cracks which will accept pitons or nuts. Using an ice axe for such work can dull its edge. An ice hammer should have a flat head, like any other type of hammer, but opposite this it should have a fairly long (5½- to six-inch) slightly curved pick which should be notched or corrugated near its tip for a secure hold in ice.

The Great Pacific Iron Works (Chouinard equipment) manufactures an ice-climbing tool called a "Climaxe," similar to an ice hammer but more like a small ice axe. It is useful for cutting steps and belay stances in steep ice, or for carving niches and alcoves in which to place ice screws and pitons. This tool does not substitute for a hammer, however, since it has no driving face.

Note that where ice pitons and screws are placed in steps and niches, there should be no bulge of ice directly in front of the pin on the downhill side. If such a bulge exists, and a carabiner is used to clip directly into the eye, it acts as a lever under heavy loading and jerks the pin out of the ice. When an ice screw or piton must be set behind a small bulge of ice which cannot be chipped away, a nylon web sling should be tied into it.

Ice hammers and small axes should be carried in belt holsters and, if equipped with shoulder slings, will not be lost if dropped.

SAFETY ON SNOW AND ICE

The ice-axe arrest and the ice-axe boot-belay are two basic and vitally important techniques on steep snow or while traveling on glaciers. Neither is applicable to ice climbing although belaying, establishing anchors, and leadership on steep ice are very similar to climbing on steep rock. For safety, ice climbing requires the use of full-length 11mm. ropes. Those of smaller diameter, such as the 9mm. or ⅜-inch, do not have sufficient margin of strength to handle severe falls, nor are their diameters great enough to provide a firm grasp with heavily gloved or mittened hands.

THE ICE-AXE SELF-ARREST

This is a method for braking and stopping a sliding fall on a steep snow slope. While it is more or less effective on snow covered with icy crust, the technique is useless on hard, black or blue water-ice. Self-arrests are also difficult, if not impossible, on steep slopes of very loose, dry, powder snow, or where the surface is so warm as to be soft and slushy. However, there is little reason to be on such unstable and dangerous terrain. The self-arrest should be practiced on smooth slopes of increasing steepness until it becomes completely automatic. Practice slopes should be free of protruding rocks or ice chunks, with a large, clear run-out at the bottom. Slopes otherwise suited to practice, but overhung by cornices or ice masses higher up, should be avoided. Find more protected areas for practice.

When climbing on steep snow, the axe is held with the thumb under the adze and the fingers and palm curled over the top of the head. The pick must be pointed to the side, well away from the body so that, if you stumble or fall forward, the pick can't be driven into your thigh or abdomen. When traversing horizontally or at a light angle up or down, the axe is held in the uphill hand. When climbing more steeply, either up or down, it can be carried in either hand.

To make a self-arrest, bring the head of the axe up quickly to your shoulder with the pick pointing to the side and slightly forward. The shaft should cross your chest at about 45 degrees, depending on your height and the length of the axe. The opposite hand grips the shaft securely near the ferrule, holding it close to the hip. This must be done instantly as you fall forward, head uphill, on to the slope. As you start to slide down, feet first, twist the head of the axe, forcing the pick deeper into the snow. Arch your back slightly to increase pressure on the pick. Be sure, too, that you keep the spike from digging into the snow, since this could stop you suddenly, flipping you head over heels, and probably jerking the axe from your grasp.

Lift your feet off the snow and keep them up until you come to a complete stop. If you fail to do this, your crampons will catch in the snow and flip you out of control, with a good chance of breaking your ankles. Lifting the feet *must* become a reflex action. The moment you hit the snow, bend your knees; keep your feet up! When you come to a full stop, jam your toes into the snow to secure your hold. Now, very carefully, get to your feet. Make sure that snow has not balled up on your crampons. If it has, clear it out with your ice axe.

Whenever climbing on snow, be ready to react instantly should you stumble or fall. If you are quick enough, there may be no need for a self-arrest. Simply slamming your pick into the snow may hold you from sliding.

However, it's wise to practice getting into a self-arrest position, no matter how you fall, or how you start to slide downhill—feetfirst on your back, headfirst on your stomach, or headfirst on your back, or any combination of these. Learn to bring the ice axe to the self-arrest position quickly no matter how you fall!

On your back with your head uphill, roll toward the head of the axe onto your stomach; headfirst on your back, you can usually pivot by dragging the spike of the axe, so that your head is uphill. As you apply pressure to the lower end of the shaft, kick your legs up and around in a close arc, pivoting around the spike where it enters the snow. This will swing you around. Sliding headfirst on your stomach, roll over onto your back and perform the same ice-axe maneuver. Remember those crampons, though. Keep your feet up! These motions must become second nature, automatic, instinctive. Figuring them out during an actual fall is too late. Wear mittens and a hat when practicing. I devote at least one full afternoon to such practice arrests and belays at the start of each climbing season.

GLISSADES

A *glissade* calls for sliding down smooth snow slopes in a sitting position, deliberately, not accidentally. The ice axe is held in the self-arrest position with the spike forced into the slope close to the hip where it acts as a brake and rudder. If you accelerate too fast, or you feel out of control, simply roll over onto your stomach and arrest the slide as I've already described. Be sure to roll toward the axe head and—again—keep your feet up until you come to a full stop. Also keep your weight on the hip closest to the spike, rather than sitting squarely on the snow, to avoid striking any possible chunk of ice or rock just below the surface of the snow. Hitting such an object with the base of your spine can result in serious injury. Standing glissades are for "hot-doggers" on mild slopes, unless snow conditions are perfect.

BELAYING ON SNOW

The sitting hip belay is the most secure, and as "bombproof" anchors *must* be established, it is—as in rock climbing—the safest. (By "bombproof" I mean one that would hold a Mack Truck going downhill in high gear.) Unfortunately, it does not readily lend itself to snow and ice climbing. As with friction climbing on rock, the generally uniform angles of snow and ice slopes make it difficult to adopt a sitting position that is both stable and reasonably convenient for the belayer, especially as he faces uphill when belaying the leader. Generally speaking, where an ice axe can be placed securely on the uphill side of a belay stance, the belayer can drop a large butterfly loop over the axe head, and with this as an anchor, belay a climber below him. His feet can be braced firmly in large bucket-steps cut into the slope. Whenever the axe is used for anchoring or belaying, place it so that the pick is uphill and the widest axis of the oval-shaped shaft is oriented in the direction of the heaviest loading. Normally, this is directly

Fig. 42. To use ice axe as belay anchor, tie butterfly knot in climbing rope and drop loop over axe. Snow must be very firm. Axe's shaft is driven in deeply and rope passes around tangs that hold head of axe to shaft. Axe's pick blade faces uphill to keep rope from slipping off.

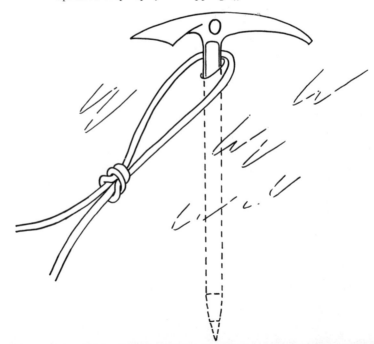

downslope from the belayer but occasionally the direction of pull may be well off to one side, possibly even upslope. This is possible if the rope is run around a large rock on which it would catch in the event of a fall, or if the rope is clipped through one or more "bombproof" points of protection upslope from the belayer.

One advantage of climbing on snow is that a small platform for a belay stance can usually be stamped into the slope or carved out with the axe. A good stance helps immeasurably when holding a hard fall. It is often possible, too, to take a belay stance which uses small crevasses or wind-scoured depressions behind or at the sides of rocks and large ice blocks. Anything you can do to increase the security of your belay is appreciated by your companions!

THE ICE-AXE BELAY

Snow slopes are often climbed continuously; that is, all members of a rope team move upward simultaneously, all at the same pace. Each climber must be ready to adopt a self-arrest position should the climber ahead stumble or fall, or if he hears a warning from the rear. Where it seems advisable to stop and belay each climber in turn, up or down the slope, the ice-axe boot belay is the most effective technique. Exceptions to this occur on extremely steep slopes, like those in narrow gullies or in couloirs, as well as on ice or snow that is too hard-packed to accept more than a few inches of the axe shaft.

Where the ice-axe boot belay can be used, stand sideways, facing as much as possible toward the climber. Kick two ample and flat-bottomed steps into the slope, one uphill about one foot in front of the other. If the snow is too hard for kick-steps, cut and scoop them out with the ice axe. On the uphill side of the upper step, force the ice axe into the snow as far as possible with the pick pointing uphill.

If the ice axe penetrates the hard subsurface layers reluctantly, drive it with your hammer, or stamp on it with your boot. If this is done, be certain later to pull the axe out in a straight line, without twisting the head, as this could break it from the shaft.

*Ascent of Mount Tressider in Alaska Range involves
direct-aid climbing on serac ice. Note vapor-barrier boots.*

Stamp the uphill foot firmly into the snow directly in front of, and touching, the shaft. The rope coming from the climber below is passed over the toe of the boot, around the shaft and back between the ice axe and the instep, and finally is held back uphill near the heel of the boot. The rope is held by the downhill hand, the fall controlled by the friction created as the rope binds on the boot and around the shaft. Friction is increased by moving the braking hand uphill above the ankle, causing the rope to slip in a sharp "S" bend. This is more secure and provides greater friction than the "C" wrap, or other variations of the ice-axe boot belay. It is, in fact, the only belay that is consistent and effective. The uphill hand must keep a firm grip on the axe head to prevent the shaft from popping out. It can be further secured by bearing down on it with the weight of your shoulders.

The belayer should consciously make the belay *dynamic* by allowing some of the rope to run through and by decelerating the fall smoothly. There's little likelihood of injury to the falling climber on snow, so that allowing some of the rope to run in order to build up friction will soften the impact on the climber, the belayer, and the ice axe. A sudden full-force stop could break the axe shaft, or jerk it out of the snow. Ideally, the belay rope should run around the shaft at the point where the rivets join the head to the shaft, but this is not always possible.

BELAYING ON ICE

Ice-axe belays are completely ineffective on ice—and extremely dangerous when attempted. Instead, belay anchors must be doubled, using two ice pitons or screws, connected so as to be self-equalizing. This is accomplished quickly and effectively by tying a Bowline on a Bight directly to the climbing rope. As in rock climbing, the rope is expected to absorb the force of a hard fall and the points of protection must be sufficiently sturdy to handle this heavy loading. Never hesitate to use rock pitons or nuts to establish solid anchors where protruding rock or containing walls along gullies present the opportunity. Falls on ice, particularly if prolonged, add the risk of damage to the rope, or of injury to other climbers via uncontrolled crampons or ice axes. Everything depends on the security of the anchor. Leading and belaying on steep ice call for techniques similar to those used on rock. Only the hardware is different. Hard, blue water-ice, formed in layers, must be climbed carefully, as it has a tendency to delaminate, with large sheets occasionally splitting off. Very early or late in the season, ice may not be securely bonded to the rock. It may even have water running under it. This can be very treacherous. Entire gullies of ice have been known to detach themselves and suddenly avalanche. Confine your climbing to areas where the ice is thick and the weather cold enough to anchor it securely to the rock. If at all possible, avoid climbing under another party. A falling axe, or climber, could seriously injure one of *your* climbers!

Member of New Hampshire Andean Expedition pauses to have his photo snapped while scaling Nevado, Tulparaju.

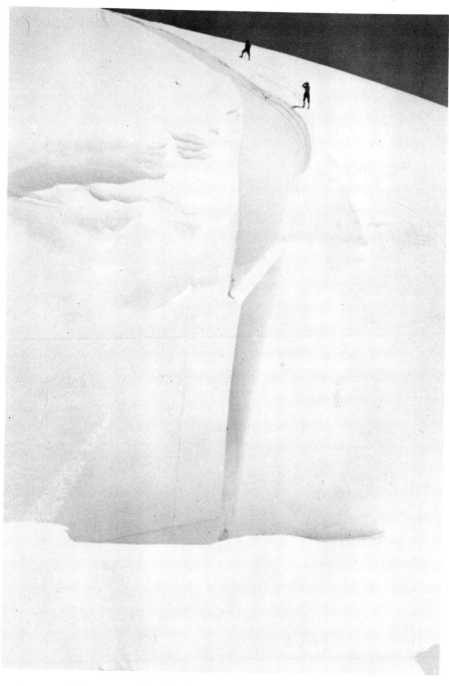

In areas with crevasses like this one on Mount Logan,
extreme caution and proper hardware are essential.

Author crosses meltwater stream on surface of
Steele Glacier during climbing expedition in Yukon.

chapter 14
Glacier Travel

Traveling on glaciers and climbing among icefalls present ultimate problems and dangers, as well as unique rewards. Along with avalanches and sudden changes in weather, crevasses are the greatest hazard. Climbing on any glacier or large snowfield, a climber risks falling into a crevasse, whether it is a narrow crack or a yawning behemoth. Before venturing onto permanent snow or ice you should know something about crevasses, where they are likely to be found, how they are formed, and how to get an unlucky climber out quickly should he fall into one. Anyone who has had this misfortune, or anyone who has

This is King Peak, as seen from 16,000-foot
altitude on Mount Logan, in heavily glaciated area.

rappeled into a crevasse for practice, is not likely to forget
the experience, nor be eager to repeat it!

Glaciers are composed of ice derived from layer upon
layer of compacted snow. Besides the ice, there are apt to
be rocks on the surface and incorporated into the ice, several layers of snow on the outer surface, and in warmer
regions during the summer, holes and tunnels full of water running under and through the glacier. For a glacier to
form, some of each season's snowfall must remain into
the next season, and then be covered by a fresh layer.

Snow more than one year old, called *firn*, or *névé*, is still porous and permeable to air and water. Glacier ice is considered to have been formed when névé reaches the point of zero permeability. This is caused by compaction from the weight of the top layers and by the gradual metamorphosis of individual snowflakes into granules of ice. These granules then fuse together and eventually form large crystals of glacial ice. Ice has physical properties characteristic of both a liquid and a solid and is, in fact, technically defined as a supercooled liquid. When glacier ice attains a depth of about 100 feet, it begins to move downhill due to the pressure of its own weight.

There are three areas on a glacier that are particularly prone to the formation of crevasses, as a result of the mechanics of glacial movement. Alpine glaciers usually occur in steep-walled, bowl-shaped *cirques*. These hollows have been cut into the mountain by the grinding and plucking action of the ice itself. Cirques have characteristically steep sides of freshly scoured rock. The first area of crevasse formation occurs where the ice pulls away from the sides and headwall of the cirque, forming a large, sometimes quite deep, crevasse known as a *bergschrund*. This is often continuous around the perimeter of the cirque and normally reaches down to bedrock. Because a bergschrund may occur on fairly steep slopes along the bottom of the cirque walls, the upper lip often overhangs the lower lip, sometimes by a considerable distance. Above the bergschrund, where the uppermost layers of snow actually meet the rock wall, there is usually a second, smaller crevasse, known as a *moat*. This is normally not difficult for climbers to cross, whereas the bergschrund may be the single most difficult problem during a given ascent.

During the summer and at the peak of the day's warmth, both the moat and the bergschrund may be nearly full of water which collects as it runs down the walls and is conducted down to the interface between the ice and the rock base. As water freezes in cracks, and along jointing planes in the rock, bits of stone are split off and become incorporated into the glacial ice. This is the manner in which a glacier steepens the headwall and enlarges the cirque. Extraordinary care, then, should be taken not to fall into water-filled, or at least wet, moats or bergschrunds. Although it may occasionally be necessary to climb down one wall of a crevasse and up the other, try to locate an area where the bergschrund is interrupted or bridged in order to avoid getting wet, or being struck by snow falling from the upper lip.

Two other areas where crevasses form on glaciers occur when the confining walls of its valley force the glacier to make a sharp bend, or when it must move over a large resistant rim or obstruction in its bed. Although ice is more or less plastic at depth, it is fairly brittle at the surface. When it must bend around a curve or move over a projection in its bed, it is subject to both stretching and compression. Stretching around the outside of a curve causes it to crack and form *crevasse fields*, while compression on the inside of a curve leads to the formation of *pressure ridges*. The folds between these ridges may appear similar to crevasses but are not normally very deep. When ice plunges down a very sharp or steep drop, *icefalls* are formed on the surface. The ice between longitudinal crevasses breaks up crosswise into blocks called *seracs*. If the glacier is active, seracs are carried to the edge, or part way down the icefall, where they often break up and collapse under their own weight. Falling seracs pose an extreme hazard to climbers and must be avoided at all cost, even if it means a long detour around the end of the ice fall.

In warmer regions, and at fairly high altitudes during the summer, the lower sections of a glacier near the *terminus* or *snout* can be morasses of slushy snow pockets and water-filled crevasses. Dry glacier surfaces which have melted back to solid glacial ice are safer and easier to walk on, since crevasses can be plainly seen. Usually, they are partially covered with stripes of broken rock, called *moraines*. This debris has been torn from the sides of cirques and valleys to be carried downstream with the ice. Streams of meltwater crisscross the surface of melting glaciers, some very deep, always cold, and often plunging suddenly into vertical wells, or *moulins*. The latter may go all the way to the glacier bed where the water flows through tunnels in the ice, or along the bedrock, to emerge at the terminus, sometimes with great force due to hydraulic pressure. Getting someone out of a moulin before he succumbs to exposure in the icy water is virtually impossible.

Because friction along the sides and *sole*, or bottom, of a glacier retards the movement of ice relative to the center, crevasses are generally distorted into crescentic curves pointing downhill. For the same reason, they are often wider and deeper at the center than at either edge. Except for the bergschrund, crevasses rarely form singly, but rather in groups. Simply because only one is visible doesn't mean that others are not close by, *hidden under the surface.*

Avalanches and blowing snow can fill crevasses solidly. More likely, though, the crevasses are bridged by wind-compacted snow. The thickness of such a bridge can

Making their way toward higher elevation, expedition members give wide berth to large crevasse on Mount Logan.

often be determined by carefully approaching an open section of the crevasse and sighting along its axis. The narrower the crevasse, the better, since the shorter a snow bridge, the sturdier it is likely to be.

Crevasses are not usually a single, long fissure but generally a series of closely spaced cracks whose ends almost meet, but not quite. In this case, it may be possible to cross safely over a vein of ice that separates two cracks. When it's not possible to determine the thickness of a bridge where you propose to cross, it can be gauged by probing with your ice axe or ski pole. Force the shaft into the snow well in front of you several times, also to either side. Do this repeatedly as you edge out over the bridge. The axe should meet considerable resistance. It may not be stopped entirely by a solid, supporting layer of compacted snow or ice, but unless some resistance is felt, chances are the bridge will collapse under your weight. Frequently, one or two men can manage to ease across a questionable bridge, only to have a third climber plunge through. You can enhance your chances of making it across by wearing skis or snowshoes since these distribute weight over a larger area. Holding your breath doesn't help!

Where willow wands are available, these can be used to mark the bridges with gates. Two wands are inserted firmly into the snow at the edges of the crevasse at either side of the bridge. The four wands form a gate clearly marking the crossing from either side of the crevasse.

ROPING UP ON GLACIERS

Venturing onto glaciers and large snowfields without being roped up is the height of poor judgment. No experienced mountaineer will succumb to the temptation to wander free and alone over smooth expanses of such ice or snow, no matter how innocent it may appear. Gigantic crevasses may lurk a few inches below the surface. Often, the only clue to a thinly bridged cavern is a minute difference in the texture of the snow's surface, or a slight variation in color which can be evaluated only by an experienced eye, and only under certain light conditions.

Author's expedition cautiously crosses Bergshrund during first ascent of Mount Tressider in Alaska Range.

During a Yukon Territory summer expedition, our party was landed on a glacier by a ski-equipped plane so that we could set up a large base camp for an extended research project. We chose a campsite, and set up tents and masts for weather instruments before dark. The pilot returned the next day with more equipment, but this time he buzzed the camp and landed several hundred yards farther away than the previous day's landing site. He lost no time in warning us. We had set up the camp directly over a huge, hidden crevasse! There was no indication of this on the surface, but from the air in that day's light, the pilot had spotted it. The day before, under different light conditions, the pilot had actually taxied across the crevasse while turning for takeoff! A few warm days under the June sun would probably have seen our camp plunged into the depths, possibly with some of the crew!

Although two men work well as a rope team on rock or ice, *three* is the minimum number for safety on glaciers. There is sound reasoning for this. If one climber of a two-man team drops into a crevasse, he'll almost certainly pull his partner in, too. Two men on the surface, however, can probably hold a third who has fallen. Three or six persons, to form two rope teams of three climbers, are a better combination than two or four men. A party of six, on two ropes, is the ideal arrangement in terms of strength, flexibility, and safety.

Author's wife is seen climbing out of enormous crevasse at 17,000 feet on Mount Logan.

Where there is the likelihood of someone's falling into a crevasse, each climber should be equipped with a *sitz-harness*, which allows him to sit comfortably with little or no weight or pressure on his waist or chest as he dangles in space. Crevasses are often deep, and overhanging lips keep the rope well out away from the walls. *This cannot be overemphasized.*

Although ⅜-inch or 9mm. ropes are often recommended for glacier travel, I prefer the extra margin of safety provided by a 7/16-inch or 11mm. line. And the larger diameters are easier to handle. A 150-foot rope is most satisfactory since it allows about 50 feet between members of a three-man team. More than 50 feet becomes unwieldy and actually increases the length of a fall due to the extra slack if team members fail to keep a nearly-taut rope. Less than 50 feet does not allow enough line for a proper belay where crevasses are wide and numerous.

Each climber should have clipped to the rope, immediately in front of himself, two *jumars* with attached step-in loops. These are mechanical, ratchet-like, one-way devices which slide free *up* the rope, but grip it firmly when weight is applied in a downward direction. The step-in loops, or stirrups, should be passed through the waist loop and tucked into a pocket or clipped to a carabiner where it can be reached easily and quickly. The pack should also be clipped to a short sling, attached to the rope or to the seat harness. Should the pack slip off during a fall, it can thus be retrieved. Also, the pack may have to be removed by a climber who has fallen into a crevasse from which he cannot climb out under the pack's weight. He can then leave the pack to be hauled out after he is rescued.

Except where snow is very wet and slushy, a rope should not be stretched so tightly between team members that it is held up in the air. A rope this taut is disconcerting for the leader, awkward and tiring on the second and third men. Sliding the rope over dry snow or ice won't hurt it.

While traveling with rope, the ice axe is held in one hand and a small coil of the rope, possibly two or three turns, in the other. It's best for all to carry the coiled rope in the same hand, keeping the rope at one side where it is less likely to be damaged by cramponed feet. Short coils are vital to flexibility and freedom of movement. For example, one team member may require enough slack for a short leap while his teammates are still plodding along with even strides.

The leader decides on the best route, avoiding crevasses if possible, and probing with his ice axe every foot of the way where these *must* be crossed. An ice-axe belay may be necessary while the leader probes a particularly dangerous spot. Snow is sometimes so soft that an ice-axe belay may be inadequate. Some other type of anchor is called for, possibly the deadman, or else snow may be cleared down to solid ice where ice screws or pitons can be set.

Inexperienced climbers frequently forget to keep the full possible distance between climbers. *This can be dangerous.* For instance, if the second man comes within a few feet of the leader, and the latter suddenly plunges into a crevasse, he may fall 50 to 60 feet, generating enough force to pull in the second man! On the other hand, if the rope has little slack, chances are the leader will fall but a few feet. Don't congregate for lunch or for a chat when crossing a glacier! Maintain the full distance allowed by the rope without actually stretching it taut.

STOPPING A FALL INTO A CREVASSE

If a climber suddenly plunges out of sight, other team members should drop immediately into a self-arrest position, facing away from the fallen climber. Should the second or third man actually see the leader fall, each or both should pivot around instantly and drive the picks of their axes into the snow. Their combined weight, plus the resistance of the axes in the snow, should stop the fall immediately. But this technique will work only if there is little, or almost no, slack in the rope!

If the man behind you falls, he'll probably shriek. Don't even look back! Fall forward into the self-arrest position, facing away from him. Once the fall has been checked, the man farthest from the crevasse should rise carefully, make sure that his partner can hold the fallen climber, then establish a solid anchor to which the weight of the climber in trouble can be transferred. Such an anchor is usually a solidly placed ice axe, perhaps even driven in with a hammer. It may be a deadman, or ice screws. In any case it must be "bombproof."

CREVASSE RESCUE

Once the fall has been stopped and the climber's weight transferred to a secure anchor, get the man out as soon as possible! Even if the temperature on the glacier's surface is well above freezing, inside the crevasse the cold is sharply penetrating. This chill will hinder the victim's efforts to use a Prussick knot or jumars as his hands stiffen. Injuries he may have suffered will be aggravated.

The simplest method of crevasse rescue calls for the climber to ascend the climbing rope under his own power with the aid of jumars. If he is unable to do this, it may be necessary to employ a more complicated process, known as the *bilgiri*, requiring two separate ropes.

The two climbers on top man the ropes, anchoring themselves securely with their ice axes. The two are designated "right" and "left," or by the color of their ropes if they differ. The climber in the crevasse stands in loops, one attached to each rope. He then signals for the ropes to be raised alternately, one step at a time. This method works well in practice, but may be difficult to set and execute in bitter cold or high wind.

If the fallen climber is injured, or so cold that he cannot help himself, he may have to be hauled out bodily. Two strong climbers may be able to lift him but, ironically, it is usually the heaviest member of the team who plunges into trouble! In this case, it is usually possible to rig a pulley system that has a mechanical advantage of two—that is, a mechanical advantage that would allow a climber to lift 200 pounds with 100 pounds of force, less a little loss due to friction. This requires two men on top, two solid anchors, and a short Prussick loop. This is not an especially fast rescue method, but it is sure, and capable of lifting a very heavy man (Fig. 43).

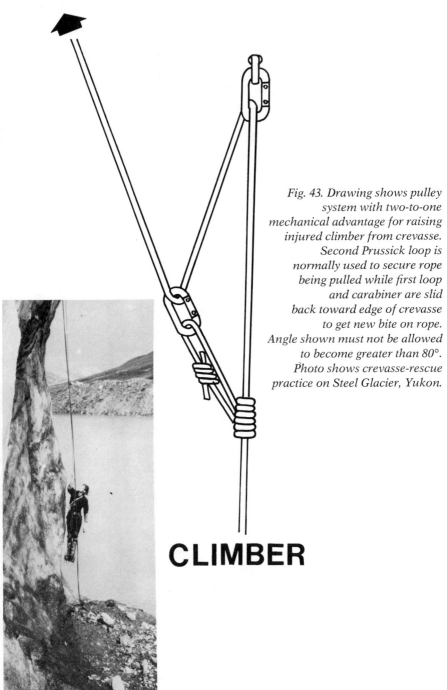

Fig. 43. Drawing shows pulley system with two-to-one mechanical advantage for raising injured climber from crevasse. Second Prussick loop is normally used to secure rope being pulled while first loop and carabiner are slid back toward edge of crevasse to get new bite on rope. Angle shown must not be allowed to become greater than 80°. Photo shows crevasse-rescue practice on Steel Glacier, Yukon.

CLIMBER

Crevasse rescue is likely to be hampered by wind, cold, poor snow conditions, and the presence of overhanging lips and cornices. Unless steps are taken to prevent it, the rope may saw its way through these overhangs so far that the fallen climber is trapped underneath. It may be necessary to chop away part of the overhang. Naturally, the trapped climber is in the fall line of the snow being cut away. Take care that no large chunks hit him. The need for this cutting away of the overhang can be minimized greatly. Before pulling the fallen climber out, insert a pack, ski pole, or axe under the rope near the edge of the lip. The rope will then run over this, rather than cut into the snow. Be sure, however, that the pack, pole, or axe is tied to some sort of anchor to prevent its falling into the crevasse during or after the rescue.

For obvious reasons, a large party is safer on glaciers than a single rope of three persons. With only three men in the party, it is in real trouble if *two* men fall into a crevasse.

Always travel at a right angle to the general orientation of the crevasse whenever possible. When you must travel parallel to several crevasses, spread out to one side or the other, so that all won't fall into the same crevasse.

Crevasse rescue cannot be learned by reading a book or studying diagrams, but should be practiced often with the same equipment you will carry during actual glacier travel. Practice should be carried out under the direction of experienced climbers who can accurately check each move for potential errors in set-up or execution. Crevasse-rescue practice should be realistic and intensive to be of real value when the need arises.

Above all, never travel on glaciers or large snowfields unless roped up to at least two other reasonably experienced climbers.

This is large ice-fall with several seracs that could tople without warning—one of greatest mountain hazards.

chapter 15
Mountain Hazards

Hazardous situations in mountaineering can be classified as *objective* and *subjective* dangers. Objective dangers are those over which the climber has no control: for example, avalanches, lightning, storms, rotten rock, unstable cornices, even bears or poison ivy. Subjective dangers, on the other hand, are those over which the climber should have immediate and direct control, examples of these being an improperly tied knot, a malfunctioning stove, a leaky canteen, lack of physical fitness, or the incompetence of companions.

At first glance it might seem easy to distinguish between the two—those hazards you can anticipate and therefore control, and those you cannot foresee or influence. The fact is that few mountain dangers are completely objective since the ultimate responsibility for being in the mountains belongs to the climber. After all, you don't have to be there. In view of this, all dangers become subjective to some degree and pretty much within the realm of your anticipation and control. A liberal use of common sense as you begin your climbing career will keep you out of trouble as you gain experience, the basis for good judgment. As you accumulate this experience, you greatly reduce your chances of coming to grief.

ROTTEN ROCK

With a little foresight, areas containing a preponderance of rotten rock can be avoided. Unlike snow, which is likely to avalanche at certain times of the day, a rockfall can occur at any time. Although climbers are occasionally injured by spontaneously falling rocks (loosened by the warmth of the sun, dislodged by a strong gust of wind or a block of falling ice) most accidents are caused by the climbers themselves. With careless movements, they send rock tumbling down, upon their own party or possibly upon another one below them.

When an area of rotten rock *must* be crossed, take precautions to prevent loose pieces from striking and possibly damaging the rope, or injuring climbers below you. Large, detached blocks, sitting on sloping ledges, are especially treacherous. Approach these only from the side and make certain that, if such a block suddenly falls, the rope is not caught under it or, worse yet, entangled with it, pulling one or more climbers along. Never climb directly over a large block or boulder on a slope, even if it appears solidly lodged. It may, in fact, be precariously balanced, ready to roll under the impact of your touch or weight! Once, in the Canadian Rockies, a block of limestone lay across our route. It was some ten feet long and four feet wide. After anchoring the rope well to one side, I gingerly pushed the rock with one hand while I clung to the cliff with the other. The merest touch of my hand did it. The rock disappeared over the side of the arête, crashing down into the valley and setting off a huge avalanche as it dislodged other rocks in its wild plunge.

Sedimentary rock, such as limestone and certain sandstones, although they can be solid, are often broken up and rotten. When climbing in areas of this type of rock, stay away from corners and ridges, and avoid climbing over the middle of concave faces of low to moderate angles. Not much loose rock is found on very steep faces since it falls as soon as loosened by frost action or by the process of exfoliation. Never attempt to climb steep, narrow gullies or couloirs where rotten rock is evident, since these are natural funnels for anything that is dislodged above. Loose and rotten rock is an extreme danger but one that can be avoided simply by climbing elsewhere.

SNOW AND ICE

Possibly more accidents occur on ice and snow than on rock because, by their very nature, ice and snow are so much more unstable than rock. Also, snowslides tend to be larger and to travel farther than rock avalanches.

Snow and ice are complex. Entire books have been written about snow avalanches and how to recognize their danger potential. Much of this information, while interesting and valuable, tends to be highly technical and somewhat impractical for mountaineers. Nonetheless, it is fairly easy to learn to recognize basic situations and snow conditions which lead to slides and avalanches.

Slightly convex slopes of low to moderate angles are more dangerous than steep faces. Snow can accumulate to a fairly great thickness before it avalanches as a result of its own weight, a rapid temperature change, or an artificial disturbance such as climbers walking on it. Snow accumulating at a rate of more than one inch per hour is likely to be unstable. Indications of this instability include "snowballing"—little cartwheels or balls rolling down spontaneously—and wind-packed snow which tends to crack into blocks, or layers which do not bond together well.

The early morning and the warmest part of the day or early afternoon are normally the most dangerous times for snow avalanches. A rapid change in the shape of the snow crystals, due to melting, may cause a slope to avalanche seemingly without cause. Occasionally a loud noise, perhaps even the shout of a climber, may trigger an enormous slide, as may a chunk of ice falling from above. Tension cracks near the top of a slope are obvious warning signals.

Never cross an open slope horizontally, or at a shallow angle. Instead, try to climb straight up, each climber following the leader's path. This reduces the chances of an avalanche by creating a vertical rather than a horizontal

Massive ice avalanche on Mount Logan crashes from Queen Peak 5,000 feet into King Trench.

line of weakness along the tracks. Ridges and corners, although they may present more difficult climbing, are usually safe from avalanches and falling ice because these tend to follow the shortest line of fall on either side of the ridge.

Travel in mountainous regions after a major storm should be restricted if possible, for at least 24 hours. This gives unstable slopes time to avalanche and it allows snow to settle and bond itself to the lower layers. Very rapid changes in weather may still initiate falls of ice and avalanches, even in areas where the snow is well consolidated and compacted. Although wind-slab and powder snow compacted by strong winds are involved in more mountaineering accidents than any other type of snow cover, all snow conditions are potentially dangerous under certain conditions. In warm weather, wet-snow avalanches and saturation slides may occur on slopes of as little as 10 degrees. These move rather slowly but when they come to a stop the high water content helps compress the snow considerably, and this is apt to freeze almost instantly, trapping a victim as if he were submerged in quick-drying concrete.

While snowslides often occur during or immediately following a storm, ice falls from glaciers at any time. Glaciers, except those in certain polar regions, move continuously, and as blocks of ice (seracs) are pushed over steeper sections of glacial bed, they collapse without warning. Climbing on a glacial icefall involves calculated risk. There simply is no predicting when a huge chunk of ice will suddenly topple, or collapse under its own weight!

Water-ice, on the other hand, is not formed from compressed snow. It is simply frozen meltwater. Such ice is found at lower altitudes in the winter and spring, particularly in New Hampshire, New York, and in the Sierra and Cascade ranges. Water-ice forms in layers which often do not bond together securely. The shock of striking such ice with an axe, or the driving of piton into it, may cause the ice to delaminate. When this happens, large sheets are apt to flake off and fall. Extreme care must be taken to protect climbers below. Establishing a belay stance well off to one side will help, and sometimes it is possible for climbers below to take shelter in an alcove or under an overhanging rock.

There are several excellent books and articles on the subject of snow, ice, and avalanches, and these are listed in the bibliography. Learn all you can about the formation of cornices, wind slab, and other unstable forms of snow and ice so that you can readily identify them in the field. As with rock climbing, avoiding danger is the best means of preventing an accident.

WEATHER

Weather, of course, is of primary importance in mountaineering. We have already seen that unstable snow conditions are the result of rapid weather changes and of storms. However, other aspects of weather contribute to the success or to the failure of a climb. Three facets of weather create hazards.

The first is wind. High wind is dangerous primarily because of its pronounced effect on exposed flesh. This is "windchill." As an example, a temperature of 10 degrees (F.) above zero combined with a 20-mile-per-hour wind (actually not a strong wind in terms of mountaineering) will cool the body as rapidly as an air temperature of 25 degrees below zero with no wind blowing! Windchill is the prime cause of frostbite injuries to skiers, climbers, and other winter outdoorsmen. Even at relatively moderate temperatures, precautions are necessary if a high wind is blowing. Adequate clothing, including facemasks and goggles, must be worn, or else travel should be restricted. There is no other solution.

A second weather hazard, one that claims the most victims among outdoorsmen in general, is cold rain. Water draws heat from the body even more effectively than cold air, and it is much more insidious. Obviously, at temperatures above freezing, there is no danger of frostbite, but cold rain can produce *hypothermia*, deadly because it lowers the temperature of the entire body, not just that of the extremities such as fingers and toes. Hypothermia is commonly known as "exposure" and results when the body's metabolism is unable to produce enough heat to cope with excessive loss while still trying to maintain the body's core warmth at a viable temperature. Frequent snacking on candy, peanuts, raisins, and other munchables will help avert this situation, providing enough sugar for use by the muscles and for conversion into heat energy.

Exposure, however, can be prevented by the simple expedient of keeping warm and dry. In cold, wet weather, a hat is necessary since as much as 40 percent of the body's heat loss can occur through the head. Wool clothing, even if wet, will help contain body warmth. Eat plenty of carbohydrates and sugars, too.

In extreme situations, where a climber's body temperature has dropped to the point where normal metabolism processes cannot reverse a continually declining temperature, additional outside warmth must be provided. Place the victim in a sleeping bag and have a second person lie in the bag with him. After the victim begins to show signs of warming up, force him to take some hot liquid, such as chocolate, well-sugared tea, or soup. If available, dextrose or other simple sugar should be added to the liquid. Severe loss of body temperature causes lethargy and sometimes disorientation or even an almost comatose state, which explains why a victim may have to be helped (or forced) to sip liquids. Nonetheless, it's important to administer something hot.

Note that it is also very important to begin by warming the victim up somewhat by means of an external heat source, such as a warm tent or the warmth of other climbers in the same bag—*before* hot liquids are administered. Otherwise there can be a sudden surge of cold blood from the extremities back into the core region of the body. If the blood from the arms and legs is cold enough, it can chill the core of the body rapidly, causing death, so you'll want to concentrate on warming up the arms and legs first.

The following articles should be required reading for all outdoorsmen who are active in winter latitudes or at high altitudes:

Hypothermia: Killer of the Unprepared, Theodore G. Lathrope, M.D., The Mazamas, 909 N.W. 19th Avenue, Portland, Ore. 97209;

Frostbite, Bradford Washburn, The Museum of Science, Boston, Mass. 02114.

The third dangerous weather situation at altitudes above 10,000 feet is, surprisingly, the opposite of the first two: strong sunlight! Especially when there is little or no wind for a cooling effect, this can be dangerous in several ways. Bright sun causes a general lassitude, a feeling of laziness, sometimes disorientation leading to a loss of judgment. This is, in effect, a mild sunstroke which can usually be prevented by wearing headgear such as a bandana, or better yet, a wide-brimmed hat with a chin strap. Dark glasses, of course, must be worn. Carry an extra pair—at the very least one extra for the party. Excessive glare may cause excruciatingly painful snowblindness, which incapacitates a person as effectively as a broken leg.

Intense sunlight at high altitudes contains a higher proportion of ultraviolet rays which can cause sunburn in a very short time. In hot weather, zinc oxide cream or a similarly effective commercial preparation should be applied to exposed areas, particularly the nose, earlobes, temples, back of the neck, and back of the hands. Lips should be protected with a special formula such as *Labiosan*. Take care, too, that the roof of the mouth and the inside of the nose are not sunburned by light reflected off the snow. Under certain conditions, severe burns to the roof of the mouth can occur and, though less commonly, to the interior of the nostrils. Learn to breathe through the nose as mush as possible. Sunburn-preventive cream will also protect the nostrils.

PHYSIOLOGICAL PROBLEMS

In addition to dangerous weather, two other hazards are associated with high altitude—*pulmonary edema* and *dehydration*. Pulmonary edema is a condition superficially resembling pneumonia. It is not caused by a micro-organism, but rather by climbing to high altitudes too rapidly. The lungs fill with fluid, hampering breathing and compounding an already strenuous situation. This can affect the heart as well and is often associated with *cerebral edema*, wherein fluid in the skull presses on vital areas of the brain. There is immediate danger of death unless the victim can be brought down rapidly to lower elevations where oxygen in the atmosphere is under higher pressure. Administering oxygen through a mask will help but not cure the condition, and if the oxygen supply runs out the victim is no better off than before. *The only remedy is to get the climber to lower altitude as quickly as possible.*

Remember that, when climbing above 12,000 to 15,000 feet, sufficient time must be allowed for the body to acclimatize fully. Pulmonary edema is a very real and constant hazard. If you are about to join a climb to such altitudes, familiarize yourself fully with the symptoms and the necessary treatment. Remember, too, that the victim of pulmonary edema may not be aware of the early stages of his condition. Climbers must, therefore, watch each other closely for symptoms.

Dehydration is the other high-altitude problem where the air is thin, cold, and extremely dry. Hard work, heavy breathing, and sweating in bright sunlight can lead to rapid dehydration. This causes muscle cramps, loss of energy, thickening of the blood leading to greater susceptibility to frostbite, and possibly even blood clots. Dehydration is common. Carry large canteens, and make frequent stops for drinking purposes. Even a liquid intake of four quarts per day may not replace moisture lost during 12 hours of climbing. Drinking only enough to satisfy your immediate thirst is not sufficient. An effort must be made to drink more than you think you need. Liquid can be taken in the form of soup, hot chocolate, fruit juices, or plain water. At lower elevations water is usually obtained easily from brooks, melting ice or snow, or rainwater pools.

OTHER HAZARDS

With the exception of being bitten by an enraged bear or chased up a tree by a bull moose, most of the common hazards in the mountains are predictable and, therefore, avoidable. Lightning, for example, does strike twice in the same place, at least in the mountains. Exposed ridges, summits, and the mouths of shallow caves are poor havens during an intense electrical storm. Apart from the possibility of being struck directly, you also run the risk of being knocked from a precarious stance, or severely burned by ground currents resulting from a nearby strike. The only safe refuge is one well down from exposed positions. Supposedly, a safe place is the hollow formed by the intersection of two slopes.

Better yet, however, get an "alpine start"—setting out early enough in the morning to complete the climb and get well down off the mountain before the afternoon storms begin to build up. These are often predictable since they are caused by warm air rising during the heat of the day to the upper levels, then condensing over the

Powder avalanches cloud face of Southeast Ridge on Dhaulagiri I in central Nepal.

peaks at cooler altitudes. In some ranges—the Tetons, for example—this is practically an everyday occurrence, so regular that "you can set your watch by it!"

Familiarize yourself, too, with noxious or poisonous plants or animals which may be present on the way to, or in the area of, a climb. Also essential when planning climbs or expeditions in foreign countries are shots and vaccinations against disease. Tetanus shots are sound insurance, and in some regions so are shots against scrub typhus or Rocky Mountain spotted fever.

In the final analysis, most hazards can be avoided by learning all you can about them and by thorough planning of your climb or expedition. Ignorance or incompetence, whether your own or that of your companions, remains the greatest hazard you face as a mountaineer. The more thoroughly you understand the mountains, their weather, wildlife, and the special conditions existing there, the safer and more enjoyable your climbing will be.

*On shoulder of Nevado Tocllaraju, members of New Hampshire
Andean Expedition prepare gear to continue climb.*

chapter *16*
Planning for Expeditionary Climbing

In time you will probably dream of more challenging climbs in the wilder and more remote regions of the world. This is the realm of expeditionary climbing. While the problems of finance, time, and accessibility may initially seem insurmountable, a full-scale expedition is not an impossible goal.

Not all expeditions are to the literal "ends of the earth," such as Patagonia, the Karakoram, or the Himalayas. What distinguishes an expedition from an extended camping trip is the greater commitment of time, money, and energy, plus the complex, far-reaching, and intensive planning and organizing that is required.

The problems and frustrations typical of the weekend climb will be encountered many times over on an expedition. In addition, the expedition will have unique problems. Many of the world's more remote and enticing climbing regions are off limits due to political reasons, military confrontations, or civil disturbances. These are often more effective in denying access to a given area than icefalls, bad weather, and rotten rock combined! Transportation and logistics may seem staggering at first, but when handled in a logical sequence, these seem to work out.

By the time you are qualified to join a major expedition, you will likely know how to plan this type of adventure. If, on the other hand, you merely want to organize a climbing trip to some remote region in a strange land, you can be guided by the logical planning steps described below.

The first consideration, of course, is the area. Develop a clear determination about the kind of climbing you want to do, then choose an appropriate region, one that holds the promise of the special conditions you require. For instance, high volcanoes rarely offer good rock climbing, whereas excellent snow and ice climbing is possible on volcanic cones whose relatively gentle slopes have been eroded by active glaciers.

Once you've decided on a peak or range, find out everything you can about it, such as political accessibility. Some governments don't like having foreigners prowling about their mountains; others welcome climbers. Obtain maps and aerial photos where possible, but don't expect these to be accurate if you're going into a relatively unexplored region for a first ascent. Part of expeditionary adventure is filling in those blank spaces on the map. In many parts of the world, even in North America, some maps are issued provisionally and have not had every detail checked for accuracy.

The next step is to determine the best means of travel. For extensive distances—more than a few hundred miles, or overseas—plane travel is almost mandatory to save time. Once closer to the goal, the travel mode can include trains, trucks, horses, even foot trekking. These are part of the adventure of the climb, and sometimes as enjoyable

*Pico de Orizaba (Citlaltepetl) in Mexico is 18,700-foot
volcanic cone—North America's third highest peak.*

as the ascent itself. Walk whenever this is feasible. However, natural barriers or a lack of time may preclude this,
in favor of a chartered helicopter or plane. Charter service
is no problem in North America and can usually be ar-
ranged in advance throughout most of the world's hinter-
lands.

Here let's interject a few words about esthetics and a
regard for the environment. Air service is expensive and
some expedition members may balk at paying for an extra
flight to bring out remaining gear after the climb, along
with unused food and trash, all of which might otherwise
be left in the mountains. Don't allow the relative ease of

*Gear and tents at well-organized expeditionary base camp
in Alaska Range show proper planning of logistics.*

approach by aircraft make you indifferent to the environment. Some charter services offer reduced rates for a "clean-up" flight. Fly out your trash!

At this stage of planning, make applications for passports, visas, insurance; and arrange for immunizations which may be required by foreign governments or your own. Apply now for travel permits where these are required. In some countries, such as Nepal, for example, climbing permits are necessary. Contact the embassies and consular offices for information.

Get a thorough physical checkup, too. Have needed dental work done to avoid having to do your own on a windswept ridge with a pair of rusty pliers! If you wear glasses, have your eyes examined if this has not been done recently. It may be time for new prescription lenses. And arrange for an extra pair to take along. These are not nuisance details but necessary steps which are part of the excitement and pleasure of planning that big trip. What's more, attention to such detail enhances your chances of a successful expedition.

The greatest planning problem is probably the selection of the expedition's members. Obviously, it's best to choose among climbers whom you know well. However, this does not mean that you must know everyone personally. This is usually impossible, since expedition members may come from all parts of the country, and may know each other

Nevado Huascaran, visited by New Hampshire Andean Expedition in 1974, is highest peak in Peru's Cordillera Blanca.

only by reputation. But don't be shy about asking for references. After all, if you are going to spend two months, or even two weeks, in the close quarters of a couple of mountain tents with a group of climbers, it's not unreasonable to feel you should all know something about each other! From a technical standpoint, some climbers have superb reputations as mountaineers, but lack the spirit, personality, or perseverance essential to success on a difficult peak.

If possible, climb at least once with each member of your proposed party before setting out—even before final plans are completed. Compatibility is vital. And, of course, you must be willing to bear the spotlight of investigation by others into *your* qualifications and general character.

The choice of a leader is critical. Anyone who resents

High-altitude porters rest with assembled gear
during American Dhaulagiri Expedition in Nepal in 1973.

Here is Mount St. Elias as seen across Seward Glacier
by Arctic Institute of North America Expedition.

being given orders is hardly leadership material, not even
qualified for expeditionary membership. The leader is
usually the climber most familiar with the area, or the one
acknowledged to be the most experienced, even if he
maintains a low profile. Each member of the team must
agree to abide by his decisions without question, barring

Base camp is set up in sunny alpine meadow during
1972 Steele Glacier Expedition in Yukon.

some extraordinary circumstance which may call for a
group consultation and decision. Otherwise, bickering
and disagreement result. I know of several expeditions
that never really got started because members could not
agree on a course of action even after arrival at the base
of a mountain. Someone *must* take the responsibility for

leading the group, or little will get done and imperative decisions will be postponed, sometimes indefinitely. Even on a day climb, someone has to decide when it's time to start back. Without this leadership, a group will often continue on past the point of no return, each member knowing full well this is wrong, yet saying nothing, assuming that the rest of the group is satisfied to continue. Someone *has* to speak up.

A leader need not be autocratic or dictatorial. Tact is part of leadership. As a rule, it is not a matter of a decision being momentous or unpopular. It's simply that *some* decision *must* be made.

Small expeditions are sometimes faced with the problem of a sudden change in plans due, possibly, to the lack of a promised aircraft, horses, or other transportation; or

This man is one of American Dhaulagiri Expedition's Nepalese sherpas, photographed by author.

long periods of bad weather; or the sudden drop-out of one member, thus reducing the party's total strength and resources. For such possibilities, have an alternative objective, acceptable to everyone. Otherwise you may end in the manner of a recent expedition to Alaska which ran into continuous foul weather. Its members couldn't agree on an alternative climb. There was bickering. The group ended up driving back home to the "Lower 48" without having climbed anything!

A large expedition—to the Himalayas, for example—has

Among greatest rewards of expeditionary climbing are
views of such majestic scenes as Nepal's Nilgiri Peaks.

greater resources and is committed to a specific objective. Small groups, however, have greater flexibility. Take advantage of this.

Once you have thoroughly mastered the basic skills of climbing, developed the art to a moderate degree, and feel confident in your ability to travel anywhere in the mountains, the whole world of climbing is open to you. There are marvelous and mysterious places waiting for those with the resolve and skill to reach them.

appendix I
Sources of Maps

In all cases, write to the appropriate agency for an index of available maps covering areas in which you are interested. This will help prevent mistakes in ordering, as well as providing you with current prices. Indexes are usually sent without charge.

UNITED STATES

United States Geological Survey (Eastern U.S.)
Distribution Section
1200 South Eads St.
Arlington, Va. 22202

United States Geological Survey (Western U.S. and
  Alaska)
Topographic Division
Building 25, Federal Center
Denver, Colo. 80225

National Ocean Survey
Distribution Division, C-44
Washington, D.C. 20235
(Write to the National Ocean Survey for an index of Operational Navigation Charts. These are small-scale, large-area maps with shaded relief covering most of the world, including some regions covered by no other maps.)

CANADA

Map Distribution Office
Department of Energy, Mines and Resources
601 Booth St.
Ottawa 4, Ont., Canada

MEXICO

Instituto de Geologia
Universidad Nacional Autonoma de Mexico
Cuidad Universitaria
Mexico 20, D.F.

OTHER COUNTRIES

National Geographic Society
16 and M Sts., N.W.
Washington, D.C. 20036

American Geographical Society
Broadway at 156th St.
New York, N.Y. 10032

John Bartholomew & Son, Ltd.
The Geographical Institute
12 Duncan St.
Edinburgh 9, Scotland

Directorate of Overseas Surveys
Kingston Rd.
Tolworth, Surbiton
Surrey, England

Institute Geographique National
107 rue La Boetie
Paris VII, France

Edward P. Stanford, Ltd.
12-14 Long Acre
London, W.C. 2, England

Reise und Verkehrsverlag
Postfach 730
Gutenbergstrasse 21
Stuttgart, Germany

appendix II
Sources of Aerial Photographs

Only U.S. and Canadian sources are listed as only these areas seem to provide extensive coverage. Other regions of the world have been photographed for special purposes but prints are difficult to obtain.

UNITED STATES

United States Geological Survey
Topographic Division
Air Photo Sales
Building 25, Federal Center
Denver, Colo. 80225

(Write first to obtain flight-line indexes covering the areas of interest. Photographs must normally be ordered by number. Often it is helpful to send along a topographic map of the area you want covered. This should be marked clearly, to help the agency locate the correct photo indexes.)

CANADA

The National Air Photo Library
Surveys and Mapping Branch
Department of Energy, Mines and Resources
615 Booth St.
Ottawa 4, Ont., Canada

appendix III
Bibliography

The following list includes atlases, accounts of classic mountaineering expeditions, and personal reflections on climbing.

Brown, Joe, **The Hard Years,** Victor Gollancz, Ltd., London, 1969

Bonnatti, Walter, **On The Heights,** Rupert Hart-davis, London, 1964

Bonington, Christian, **I Chose to Climb,** Victor Gollancz Ltd., London, 1969. Also **Annapurna South Face.**

Crew, Peter, **Dictionary of Mountaineering,** Arthur Barker, London, 1968

Harrer, Heinrich, **The White Spider,** Dutton, New York, 1960

Herzog, Maurice, **Annapurna,** Dutton, New York, 1960

Hiebeler, Toni, **North Face in Winter,** Lippincott, Philadelphia, 1963

Manning, Harvey, Editor, **Mountaineering: The Freedom of the Hills,** The Mountaineers, Seattle, Wash. 1967

Maraini, Fosco, **Karakorum, The Ascent of Gasherbrum IV,** Hutchinson, London, 1961

Milne, Malcolm, **The Book of Modern Mountaineering,** Arthur Barker, London, 1968

Moore, Terris, **Mt. McKinley: The Pioneer Climbs,** University of Alaska Press, Fairbanks, 1967

Noyce, Wilfred and McMorrin, Ian, **World Atlas of Mountaineering,** MacMillan, New York, 1970

Rebuffat, Gaston, **Mount Blanc to Everest,** Studio, New York 1956

Rebuffat, Gaston, **Starlight and Storm,** Dent, London, 1956

Rebuffat, Gaston, **Men and the Matterhorn,** Oxford University Press, New York, 1965

Rebuffat, Gaston, **On Snow and Rock,** Oxford University Press, New York, 1968

Roberts, David, **The Mountain of My Fear,** Vanguard Press, New York, 1968

Sayre, Woodrow Wilson, **Four Against Everest,** Prentice-Hall, Englewood Cliffs, N.J., 1964

Shipton, Eric, **Mountain Conquest,** Harper and Row, New York, 1966

Slesser, Malcolm, **Red Peak,** Coward-McCann, New York, 1964

Ullman, James Ramsey, **Americans on Everest,** Lippincott, Philadelphia, 1964

Wall, David, **Rondoy,** John Murray, London, 1965

appendix IV
Specialized Books and Articles on Mountain Medicine

Lathrope, Theodore G., M.D., **Hypothermia,** Mazamas, Portland, Ore.

Trott, Otto T., M.D., **Improvised First Aid for Severe Mountaineering Injuries,** appearing in OFF BELAY, Jan.-Feb. 1972, Vol. 1.

Washburn, Bradford, **Frostbite,** Boston Museum of Science, Boston, Mass.

Committee on Injuries, **Emergency Care and Transportation of The Sick and Injured,** American Academy of Orthopedic Surgeons

Field, Ernest K., Editor, **Mountain Search and Rescue Operations,** Grand Teton Natural History Association, Moose, Wyo.

Wilkerson, James A. M.D., Editor, **Medicine for Mountaineering,** The Mountaineers, Seattle, Wash.

Books and Articles Dealing with Snow Conditions

LaChapelle, Edward R., **Field Guide to Snow Crystals,** University of Washington Press, Seattle, 1969

Mellor, Malcolm, **Avalanches,** Cold Regions Research and Engineering Laboratories, Hanover, N.H. 1968

Roch, Andre, **Avalanches,** The Mountain World, 1962-63, Rand McNally Co.

LaChapelle, Edward R., **The ABC of Avalanche Safety,** Colorado Outdoor Sports Corp., Denver, Colo.

appendix V
Glossary
of Terms

AID CLIMBING Also known as sixth-class or direct-aid climbing, this method requires the use of pitons, chockstones, and various types of "nuts" jammed into whatever cracks are available. To these are attached steps, or etriers, made of knotted nylon webbing. The purpose of these is to provide hand- and footholds over extremely difficult or blank sections of the rock. Normally, in other types of climbing, only what natural foot-and handholds the rock provides are used. Aid climbing is sometimes done on very steep or overhanging ice. In this case, ice screws or ice pitons replace the other types of anchors and the etriers are attached to them.

ANCHOR As used by climbers, this word can be either a verb or a noun. An anchor is anything the climber attaches himself to in order to keep from being pulled off the mountain should his partner, to whom he is connected by the rope, fall. Often this is a piton or chocknut, occasionally a sling wrapped around a large, stable block, an ice screw or, where available, a stout, healthy tree. To "anchor" to attach yourself securely to the mountain. If the anchor is not "bombproof" it is virtually useless.

BELAY Literally this means to seize and secure and the word is derived from the days of sailing ships when running lines, rigging, and sails were said to be "belayed," or held fast. A sail, for example would be held taut with a rope snubbed around a belaying pin. In climbing, belaying means to protect the climber from falling, at least very far, by constantly keeping the rope under control and in a position so that it can be instantly snubbed and held tightly to arrest the fall.

BERGSCHRUND A crack or crevasse, often quite large, that separates the ice of an alpine glacier from the rock of the mountain itself. It is caused by the ice constantly pulling away from the rock as it moves slowly downhill under its own weight. It is usually difficult to cross, as the upper lip is higher and sometimes overhangs the lower lip.

CARABINER A more or less oval metal ring with a spring-loaded gate in one side. It is used to clip the climbing rope to another rope or to a fixed anchor, or wherever the rope must be securely attached to something while still allowing it to slide freely.

CRAMPONS Rigid or hinged metal frames with 10 to 12 points, ¾″ to 1½″ long. These fit over the climbing boots and are strapped on with nylon or neoprene straps. They allow the climber to gain purchase on steep snow or ice.

ETRIERS Small, portable steps or ladders made of nylon webbing. Usually they have three steps and are made of 1″-wide nylon webbing. They are used in direct-aid climbing to provide hand- and footholds where none are available on the rock itself.

FIXED ROPE A rope that is permanently attached to a sound anchor to provide, normally, a quick and relatively safe descent or ascent over a dangerous or difficult section of rock or snow that must be climbed several times. Fixed ropes are most often used on expeditionary climbs at higher altitudes where many separate trips must be made to carry food and supplies to higher camps. The function is basically that of a safety line.

HARDWARE A collective term for pitons, carabiners, nylon slings, chocknuts and other equipment that a climber carries to provide protection or establish anchors. The term is applied to both rock- and ice-climbing equipment.

ICE HAMMER A medium-weight hammer with a long curved pick on one end of the head and a flat hammer head on the other. The face of the hammer is used for driving pitons into the ice and the pick is used for chopping, gaining purchase in the ice like a large claw, and providing leverage for turning ice screws in, or out.

ICE PITON A long, usually flat piece of steel (up to 2 feet long) with an eye on one end and barbs on the other. There are several varieties.

ICE SCREW Usually a medium-length, tubular piece of metal with an eye on one end and a short section of coarse threads on the other. Normally these are hammered slightly into the ice, then turned in the rest of the way with the pick of the ice hammer.

JUMAR A metal clamping device that works on a cam principle to grip the rope securely. It can easily be pushed up a hanging rope but the cam will not allow it to slide back down. Jumars are normally used in sets of two with nylon etriers attached. They are all but essential for crevasse rescue and for ascending steep, fixed ropes.

NUTS A collective term for all the artificial metal or plastic wedges and chockstones that a climber uses to provide anchors when climbing rock. Often these can be used instead of pitons and are preferable because they can be placed rapidly, do not damage the rock as pitons often do, and can be removed by the second climber more easily than pitons (in most cases, that is).

OBJECTIVE DANGER A danger over which the climber has little or no control. Examples would be lightning, storms, high wind, rotten rock, high altitude. Precautions can be taken to minimize these dangers but they can never be eliminated entirely.

PICKETS Aluminum pipes, or T-sections, usually 3 to 4 feet in length and about 1⅜ inches in diameter. These are normally equipped with a short nylon sling and take the place of ice screws in snow that is too soft to hold other types of anchors. They are very often used in pairs.

PITCH The distance the leading climber climbs before stopping to anchor and belay the second man up to his stance. Normally this would be approximately a hundred feet or a little more. A pitch can be any length, however, and often must be shorter or longer depending on the type of rock being climbed and the availability of belay stances. The term is also used in snow and ice climbing, though in this type of climbing pitches tend to be more uniform in length.

PITONS Metal blades and wedges with an eye on one end. Pitons are driven into cracks in the rock with a hammer and provide sound points of attachment for the rope by clipping it into the eye with a carabiner. Many shapes are available for use in different cracks. A piton is normally removed by the last man on the rope, by hitting back and forth along the axis of the crack.

PITON HAMMER A short, medium-weight hammer used for driving and removing pitons. In most popular models the handle is of hickory to give the proper balance. It is usually equipped with a shoulder sling of nylon webbing to prevent loss if dropped.

PRUSSICK KNOT A special type of hitch, not really a true knot. The prussick is used to allow a good grip on the slippery nylon climbing rope. Normally it is used for climbing fixed lines, but it has a multitude of other uses, especially in rescue work. When tied correctly, it can be pushed either way on a rope but when tension is applied it grips the rope firmly and resists sliding.

RAPPEL (ABSEIL) A controlled sliding descent down a single or, more often, a double rope. Friction to brake and control the rate of descent is obtained either by wrapping the rope around the body (under one thigh, across the chest and over the opposite shoulder) or by means of a braking system rigged with carabiners.

SCREE Small stones and gravel that are often found on mountain slopes below snowline, particularly on the sides of volcanic cones. Scree is kept out of the boots by elastic "scree collars," anklets, or gaiters.

SEAT HARNESS A diaper-seat arrangement made of wide nylon webbing similar to that used in automotive seat belts. It is usually stitched together with strong nylon thread and fastened with a heavy metal buckle. It resembles the lower part of a parachute harness. It is often used where the climber must spend considerable time dangling from fixed ropes on vertical or overhanging walls. This type of harness is also very useful in areas where there is danger of falling into a crevasse. It eliminates strain on the waist but is heavier, more complicated, and reduces the sense of grace and freedom on less severe rock. Some climbers hate seat harnesses and some can't get along without them.

SERAC A large block of glacial ice, formed as a glacier descends over a steeper or rougher section of its bed. Seracs are notoriously dangerous because they often suddenly collapse under their own weight, sometimes causing massive ice avalanches onto the lower parts of the glacier.

SLINGS Small loops of nylon cord or webbing, anywhere from a few inches to several feet in length. They are used for rigging anchors, tying into something temporarily, carrying equipment and a multitude of other uses on technical climbs.

SUBJECTIVE DANGERS A danger over which the climber ought to have immediate and direct control. Examples would be an improperly tied knot, a leaky canteen, missing components in a first-aid kit, going to high altitudes too quickly to allow full acclimatization, and the incompetence of one's companions. There are, unfortunately, many, many more.

SWAMI BELT A length of nylon webbing, 1″ wide by approximately 15 feet long, that is wrapped around the waist by any of several different methods and secured with a water knot. Its function is to provide a nonstretching, wide belt or band around the climber's body on which to attach the climbing rope. This provides an independent tie-in that is more comfortable in the event of a fall and allows more of the climbing rope to be used for belaying.

TALUS An accumulation of large and medium-sized pieces of rock at the foot of cliffs and at the bottom of couloirs and gullies. The rock is derived from broken pieces wedged off the terrain above by frost action and exfoliation.

WHITE-OUT Conditions of fog, or blowing snow, or any combination that makes it impossible to tell earth from sky, even relatively close to you. A similar condition is sunlight filtered through thick fog or mist that produces lighting so flat it is impossible to detect minor undulations in the snow surface. Even foot prints are occasionally so difficult to see that they can only be detected by feeling for them with the hand. In dangerous terrain, travel should be restricted during a white-out.

WILLOW WANDS On glaciers or extensive snow-covered areas, willow wands are used to mark a safe route through crevasse fields, or over the shortest, safest line between camps. Rarely are they actually of willow. More likely they will be 3- to 4-foot bamboo wands of the type used to stake up tomato plants in the garden. Fluorescent orange paint or attached strips of bright plastic aid in making them visible in conditions of white-out or storm. Normally they are placed one rope length apart, not further. Double wands are used to mark safe routes over snow bridges, sharp turns in the trail, etc.

Index

Note: Page numbers in italics indicate illustrations.